Your Book
in Print

Your Book

HOW CUSTOM PUBLISHING CAN WORK FOR YOU

in Print

ATHENA DEAN

UPWRITE BOOKS

A Division of WINEPRESS PUBLISHING

UpWrite Press (a division of WinePress Publishing, PO Box 428, Enumclaw, WA 98022) functions only as book publisher. As such, the ultimate design, content, editorial accuracy, and views expressed or implied in this work are those of the author.

Unless otherwise noted, Scripture quotations are from the *New King James Version* of the Holy Bible. Copyright © 1979, 1980, 1982. Used by permission of Thomas Nelson, Inc. Scripture versions marked NLT are taken from the New Living Translation of the Bible.

Previously published under ISBN 1-883893-82-8 as *You Can Do It! A Guide to Christian Self-publishing.*

ISBN 13: 978-1-4141-1244-2
ISBN 10: 1-4141-1244-0
Library of Congress Catalog Card Number: 2008928265

To the many Christian writers scattered across the country who have—through their questions, concerns, and stories—inspired me.

Publish his glorious deeds among the nations.
Tell everyone about the amazing things he does.
—Psalm 96:3, NLT

Contents

Introduction

. . . .

I LOOKED FRANTICALLY around the plush lobby of the Sheraton Inn Atlanta. The billboard listed many events, but the Christian writers' conference at which I was supposed to be speaking was not one of them.

"All things work together for good" came quickly to my mind. I dismissed that thought impatiently and thought, *Oh sure, God . . . here I am, stranded!* The nightmare of an overfull calendar colliding with reality had come true. I had written the dates for the conference incorrectly in my day planner and was now in the right place at the wrong time. I could feel a lump rising in my throat. I had worked so hard to get everything done so I could be away from the WinePress office for four days. Now I was confronted with the fact that I was in a strange hotel, with nothing to do and a nonrefundable plane ticket that forced me to stay over Saturday night. The front desk clerk was nice enough to give me the "airline rate" for my room. When I finally got up there, I fell to my knees.

Oh, Jesus! Why am I here? How could this have happened? What is going on?

Ever so gently, that still, small voice whispered into my heart, "You've been asking me for time to write, haven't you?"

The light came on . . . fireworks went off . . . the choir started singing, "Glory, Glory, Hallelujah!" *That's it!* I had spent my whole flight to Atlanta scribbling an outline for the book you are holding in your hand. Above the quiltwork patches of Midwestern farms, I had fine-tuned the outline and had discussed it with God.

Lord, when am I ever going to have time to write this book? I know I need to, and I know You want me to—but Lord, when? I didn't get an answer, but I continued writing down ideas.

Christian writers' conference directors had been after me for six months to put into print the concepts I had learned firsthand in the Christian publishing business He'd led me to establish in 1991 and that I taught in my classes. There has been a need for information about self-publishing specifically geared to the Christian market, and many felt that God was going to use me to fill that need.

Within hours I had arranged for a computer and printer to be delivered to my hotel room, along with a carafe of hot coffee. Two long, grueling days (and more coffee) later, I emerged from room 310, disk in hand—mission accomplished! Well, at least the first draft of the mission.

God, in His infinite mercy, arranged my circumstances to give me both the time to write the book and the energy to complete it. It was a miracle out of misery. My prayer is that through this book many more miracles will come and many believers will be helped to get their work into print.

Since the first edition of this book was printed under the title, *You Can Do It,* I've watched the Christian publishing industry move toward focusing on celebrities and cutting back on titles from new authors. Even authors who have been in the publishing industry for years say it's challenging to earn a living as a Christian writer. One prolific, well-known author regularly received reports from friends who couldn't find her books in Christian bookstores. Frustrated and disillusioned, she felt like quitting. Getting the elusive contract with a big publisher is not all it's cracked up to be.

The good news? Such changes in the publishing industry only make self-publishing a much more viable option. WinePress Publishing is blessed by the Lord to be the recognized leader in this cutting-edge trend.

I've added some great new material to this new book. You'll find tips for how to raise the money to fund your project and how to get the most out of the media. The "how to do it yourself" information included in previous editions has been removed for good reason. Many authors try to cut costs by doing their own editing, cover design, and printing. The result: more books look self-published, which makes it challenging for the Christian self-publishing market to maintain a respectable reputation. I no longer recommend that anyone go it alone. Instead, I urge you to use a *reputable* book packager—one who has a long track record of producing quality product and offering many options to the author.

In this edition I have deleted mention of other companies. Thanks to our executive publisher, WinePress now has a no-gossip policy. When it comes to talking about our competitors, we make a point to leave names out, so you'll see many instances where a quote or comment involves the name of a competitor and I've replaced it with *** or brackets with a generic term such as [secular POD publisher].

Introduction

Believe me, I could talk for days about the stories I hear about other companies, but I'd rather ensure that my religion is not worthless (James 1:26) and only speak those things which will build others up according to their need (Ephesians 4:29).

It is my prayer that the information provided in this new and expanded edition blesses you and enables you to finish the race the Lord has given you to run, getting your message out in a way that effects eternity forever.

CHAPTER 1

Why Self-Publish?

• •

HAS THE LORD given you a message? Yes? Then why haven't you published it yet? I can almost hear your answer: "I can't find a publisher interested in my book. I keep getting rejection slips." That stack of rejection slips may have little to do with the quality of your writing—or the significance of your message. But it has everything to do with trends in the Christian publishing industry.

A publishing industry proverb says: "For every 100 people who say they're going to write a book, one starts a book. For every 100 people who start writing a book, one finishes a book. And for every 10,000 books that are finished, one gets published."

That proverb isn't far off the mark. Consider the manner in which publishing companies do business. Some publishers believe in publishing a multitude of titles with the expectation of decent sales for all. Others believe in publishing fewer titles with the expectation of high sales volumes for each one. Most Christian publishing companies follow the second trend—fewer titles with higher sales volume.

The Blockbuster Mentality

Christianity Today magazine reports that Christian publishing has enjoyed a string of Godzilla-sized hits in recent years—starting with the Left Behind series (with a sales of more than 60 million copies), followed by *The Prayer of Jabez* (more than 9 million copies sold), *The Purpose-Driven Life* (30 million copies sold), *90 Minutes in Heaven* (1.5 million copies sold), and *Blue Like Jazz* (1 million copies sold).[1]

Most Christian publishers focus on potential blockbusters. Mostly, it's a matter of economics. Across the board, books published by royalty publishers do not earn back their advances.

During the past 20 years, book prices have increased by more than 35 percent.[2] In 1980, the average hardcover book cost about $15. In 1997, the price jumped to $24.[3] From 1997 to 2008, book prices increased another 14.4 percent.[4] High paper costs limit the number of books publishers can afford to publish each year, so they focus on titles guaranteed to give them the biggest bang for their buck.

"We desire not to publish books that sell just 10,000 or 20,000 units . . . it takes almost as much effort to sell 10,000 as 200,000," says Michael Schatz of Multnomah Books,[5] (this article came out before Multnomah was sold to Random House in 2006).

At the Mt. Hermon Christian Writers' Conference one year, I attended a workshop taught by an editorial representative from a major Christian publishing house. He revealed that they receive 24,000 unsolicited manuscripts per year and publish only 12-to-17 new titles annually.

A director of sales from another large Christian publishing house told me they receive as many as 3,000 manuscripts per year and publish approximately 150 titles. He told us, "Many of those wonderful efforts find other publishers, but sadly, many never find a home."

Al Hsu, an acquisitions and development editor at InterVarsity Press, told *Christianity Today* that good books with less commercial potential "get squeezed out of the market and displaced from bookstore shelves to make way for high-profile books that publishers need to sell a boatload of to break even on."[6]

Editors explain that the authors to whom they offer contracts "have to bring something to the table." That "something" includes:

1. A unique, cutting-edge topic that fits into a particular publisher's niche
2. A Ph.D. or other certified training that establishes the author as an authority in his or her area
3. Strong communication skills and/or the ability to speak in front of large crowds
4. A built-in audience stemming from an established speaking ministry, regular media exposure, or a mail-order ministry that would purchase 10,000-to-20,000 copies a year (to resell at speaking engagements)

Those expectations rule out many Christian writers. However, just because you may not fit into the narrow criteria of a major publishing house doesn't mean the message God has given you shouldn't be in print. But you must be realistic. You need to look at the cold, hard facts of Christian publishing and evaluate your chances of selling your work to a major Christian publisher.

Bruce Zabel, a long-time publishing industry professional, shared several additional trends during an interview for our WinePress newsletter:

Agents

One of the growing practices and trends is for publishers to use agents, like myself, to do their screening for them. I get a thousand to two thousand ideas or proposals yearly and I reject 99 percent of those . . . of the 1 percent I submit to publishers, only a fraction get serious consideration. Some publishers look at unsolicited manuscripts, but it is becoming more and more rare. Most won't even talk to a writer unless he or she has an agent, and writers generally don't pick an agent—the agent picks them!

Celebrity Authors

The bigger publishers—and you can't fault them for this—would rather contract with an author who has a proven track record and is a proven seller. So it's rare for them to publish an unknown author. It does happen, but not too often.[7]

"Books by sports stars, entertainers, or other icons of the pop culture—a significant number of which are ghostwritten—have become big sellers for Christian publishers," writes Gene Veith in WORLD magazine.[8]

At another large writers' conference, a senior editor from Thomas Nelson noted that celebrities get most of their attention. The editor shared that it comes down to dollars and cents: If they aren't absolutely sure they can move 25,000 hardcover copies of a book in the first year, they aren't interested.

At a Christian writers' conference in Pennsylvania, the editorial director for Thomas Nelson was the keynote speaker. He told the audience that Thomas Nelson looks for "luminaries"—the professional athlete, gospel singer, or preacher/teacher who is already famous. They want a star who can move 25,000–50,000 copies during the first five months after a book's release.

"Consider the example of Hollywood," writes Collin Hansen in Christianity Today. "Movie studios would sooner take their chances on a star-studded cast with an iffy script than an unknown actor with a promising concept. It's a safer bet. Likewise, some Christian publishers cast their lot with authors whose faces they can slap on the front of a book."[9]

I had the opportunity to spend time with an acquisitions editor who has worked for some of the biggest Christian publishers during the last 20 years. She frankly told me that she struggled with promising new authors the moon when she knew that the publishers allowed her to sign them on only to fill empty spots in the catalog. All the marketing dollars were spent on the big names. Once the catalog was replaced with the next season's catalog, the new authors' books were taken out of print and forgotten about. It is sad that Christian publishing has come to the point of using new authors as filler.

The same trend is prevalent within the general publishing market. Publishers need book sales to cover the costs of the author's contract, printing, production time (editors, artists designing the dust cover, etc.), and shipping.

> Outlandish advances to celebrity authors have drained publishers' pockets, and more often than not, the [celebrity authors'] subsequent books don't sell nearly as well as expected. The only way publishers can make up such losses is to cut back on contracts with lesser-known writers. Those authors are lumped into the "mid-list" category, meaning that their often well-written books regularly sell 5,000 to 10,000 copies. (It takes sales of 50,000 to 60,000 to make most bestseller lists.)
>
> That doesn't mean that the publishers lose money on those modestly selling books. Despite the millions thrown to celebrities, most working writers rarely exceed $5,000 in royalty advances. If their books sell 10,000 copies, the publishers will probably make a profit.
>
> So why don't publishers simply abandon the expensive celebrities and concentrate on talented, less-compensated authors? Because the chain bookstores can buy titles in bulk and offer substantial discounts from the suggested retail price. And chain bookstores want books by big-name authors.[10]

First-Time Authors

If you find it hard to believe that publishers are most interested in big-name authors, pick up a copy of the *Christian Writers' Market Guide* by Sally Stuart. Each publisher includes information about the percentage of first-time authors they publish. Sadly, the percentages are almost always very low, and have worsened since the original printing of this book in 1996.

I speak regularly at Christian writers' conferences, and I am concerned with the message several better-known authors promote. They say things like, "Don't quit; if I can do it, you can do it. I just signed a three-book contract with a major publisher before writing the manuscripts . . . I work in my sweats, in the comfort of my own home, and I set my own hours. I am a full-time Christian writer. It took me fifteen years to get to this place, but if I can do it, every one of you can, too."

I agree that if God has given you the gift or burden for writing, you should do all you can to perfect your craft, and you should be persistent. But such comments fan unrealistic expectations into flame. It's debatable that your name will be in lights just because you keep at it for fifteen years.

Secular Conglomerates

One explanation for why the largest Christian publishers have shifted their focus to big names is that many of them are owned by secular corporations or have shares held by Wall Street investors:

- Random House acquired Multnomah and WaterBrook (now known as WaterBrook Multomah Publishing Group). Random House also owns Shaw Books (an imprint of WaterBrook Press).
- Simon & Schuster acquired Howard Publishing (now called Howard Books).
- Media magnate Rupert Murdoch (whose holdings include Fox, Harper-Collins, MySpace, and TV Guide), owns Zondervan.
- Hachette Book Group owns FaithWords (formerly known as Warner Faith).
- InterMedia Partners merged with Thomas Nelson.
- The Wicks Group owns Standard Publishing.

General trade publishers such as Penguin Putnam have also launched "spiritual" imprints (Riverhead Books) and Christian imprints (Penguin Praise). The consolidation of so many formerly independent publishing houses results in "increased influence on business decisions by bean counters and lawyers instead of traditional book people," writes F.W. Baue in WORLD Magazine.[11]

At the 2004 Mount Hermon Christian Writers' Conference, Dr. Rosalie de Rossett, Professor of Literature at Moody Bible Institute, noted:

> Walk into the brightly-colored packaged clutter of the nearest bookstore and what do you see? Movie star gossip, secrets of the pyramids, stock market guides to better health and body size, confessions of accomplished swindlers and convicted murderers, beauty tips from actresses famous and not-so-famous, and any number of other ephemeral pursuits.
>
> Ironically, the more subtle the author's thought and the more careful his argument, the smaller his chance of notice . . . The shoddy work sells as well as—or better than—the good work . . . If you walk into Christian bookstores, the picture, sadly, is often not very different, though the approach is described as 'Christian.'

The compulsion to cater to convenience-minded consumers, rather than focusing on evangelism and sound doctrine—has invaded the Christian publishing industry, particularly among publishers owned by secular media magnates. Some of these publishers push "crossover" books—Christian titles that have a strong potential to sell well in the general market.

For better or for worse, the Christian publishing industry follows the trends of the secular publishing market. When something big hits in the secular publishing world, you're likely to see a Christianized version in religious stores six months later. "Romances, horror novels, management books, and other popular genres that are essentially written according to easy-to-follow formulas rather than original insights, all have their counterparts in Christian bookstores," writes Gene Edward Veith in *WORLD* Magazine.[12]

The Christian publishing industry is rife with books written by pop psychologists and motivational speakers.

> "Our culture's obsession with physical beauty gives rise to Christian diet plans and Christian exercise videos. Even when it comes to religion, Christian publishing often follows trends rather than leads, as in the rash of books on angels and near-death experiences inspired by New Age books on the same subjects," continues Veith.[13]

And, of course, the secular media giants are most interested in showcasing big-name authors who write in the "popular" style, which leaves many mid-list authors (those who sell 5,000-to-10,000 copies) and almost all new authors out in the cold.

Chain Stores

In the same manner, Christian chain stores and retail franchises are swallowing up many independent, family-owned bookstores. These "big box" retailers can buy huge quantities of books and supply their stores with deeply discounted products. However, they, too, focus on stocking fewer titles—those that result in the biggest sales.[14]

Not only that, but books take up very little space in Christian "bookstores" these days. Walk in to your local Christian store (many are no longer called "bookstores") and you'll find three quarters of the shelves brimming with music CDs, videos, art, clothing, greeting cards, games, and gift items. You'll find a few books, too, but mostly, the books on the shelf are the ones projected to be top sellers.

The Self-Publishing Option

Given the current direction of Christian publishing, self-publishing may be your only option. And it could be a good one, too. *Writers Digest* predicted that the publishing industry is moving toward an increase in titles, lower print runs, and more print-on-demand books (a technology that allows books to be printed a few at a time).[15]

Consider this article excerpted from *U.S. News & World Report*:

> Former Milwaukee salesman Fred Gosman couldn't interest a publisher in his book on why parents should stop spoiling their kids. "You're no expert," he was told. But Gosman figured that being a parent was expertise enough. So, after being rejected by twenty or so publishers, he decided he would publish *Spoiled Rotten: Today's Children and How to Change Them* on his own.
>
> Gosman, whose book has since sold tens of thousands of copies, is in good company. "Self-publishing is the fastest-growing segment of the publishing industry," says Jan Nathan of the Publishers Marketing Association [PMA] trade group.[16]

Industry professional Bruce Zabel, who highlighted trends in the publishing industry earlier in this chapter, says of self-publishing:

> If you have a forum from which to sell your books, or a "built-in" market, it could work out for you. You just can't publish books and not have a way to get them to people who might want them. Second, if you have the time and inclination to invest in selling and marketing your books, either as a part-time or a full-time business, then it could be a very viable way to go.

Many self-published authors are surprised to learn that their biggest job begins after their book is printed.

> *Spoiled Rotten* author, Gosman, lived in his car and in cheap motels for weeks, pitching his book to newspapers, radio, and television. Gosman's grueling schedule paid off when the publicity led to an offer from Villard Books (a subsidiary of Random House), and an advance in the high five figures.
>
> Craig Zirbel, who wrote *The Texas Connection: The Assassination of John F. Kennedy*, credits providence for his stints on the New York Times and other best-seller lists. "It's like I was sitting in the ballpark waiting for the game and someone threw me the ball and I hit a grand slam. It's pure dumb luck."[17]

You and I know it's not about luck—it's about hearing God and being obedient to what He tells us to do. When we obey, He blesses. Bruce Zabel says, "I have known some self-publishing ventures that have been very successful. Authors have gone to an organization like WinePress that helped them edit, stylize, typeset, and print their book. In this way they have gotten it into presentable form, which is crucial. Then they turned around and sold those books and made a good profit. They were able to see lifelong dreams come true. Their message was in print and selling."

Dan Poynter's best-selling book, *The Self-Publishing Manual*, 14th Edition (Para Publishing 2003) gives us eight good reasons to self-publish:

1. *To make more money.* Why accept 6 percent to 10 percent in royalties when you can have 35 percent? You know your subject and you know the people in the field. Certainly you know better than some distant publisher who might buy your book. While the trade publisher may have some good contacts, he doesn't know the market as well as you, and he isn't going to expend as much promotional effort. Ask yourself this question: Will the trade publisher be able to sell four times as many books as I can?

2. *Speed.* Most publishers work on an 18-month production cycle. Can you wait that long to get into print? Will you miss your market? The 1 ½ years don't even begin until after the contract negotiations and contract signing. Publication could be three years away! Why waste valuable time shipping your manuscript around to see if there is a publisher out there who likes it?

3. *To keep control of your book.* According to *Writer's Digest*, 60 percent of the big publishers do not give the author final approval on copy editing. Twenty-three percent never give the author the right to select the title, 20 percent do not consult the author on the jacket design and 36 percent rarely involve the author in the book's promotion. The big New York trade publishers may have more promotional connections than you, but with a stable of books to push, your effort may get lost in the shuffle. The big publishers are good at getting books into bookstores but they fail miserably at approaching other outlets. Give the book to someone who has a personal interest in it—the author.

4. *No one will read your manuscript.* Many publishers receive more than 100 unsolicited manuscripts for consideration each day. They do not have time to unwrap, review, rewrap and ship all these submissions. Unless you are a movie star, noted politician or have a recognizable name, it is nearly impossible to attract a publisher. Many publishers work with their existing stable of authors and accept new authors only through agents.

5. *Self-publishing is good business.* There are more tax advantages for an author-publisher than there are for just authors.

6. *Self-publishing will help you to think like a publisher.* You will learn the industry and will have a better understanding of the big picture. A book is a product of one's self. An analogy may be drawn with giving birth. The author naturally feels that his book is terrific and that it would sell better if only the publisher would dump in more promotion money. He is very protective about his book (ever try to tell a mother her child is ugly?). The publisher answers that he is not anxious to dump more money into a book that isn't selling. So, if the author self-publishes, he gains a better understanding of the arguments on both sides. It is his money and his choice.

7. *You will gain self-confidence and self-esteem.* You will be proud to be the author of a book. Compare this to pleading with people to read your manuscript.

8. *Finally—you may have no other choice.* There are more manuscripts than can be read. Most publishers don't have time to even look at your manuscript.[18]

I'd like to add one more compelling reason to self-publish. The more commercial and worldly the Christian publishing industry becomes, the harder it is to get books that address controversial topics published. My books on the dangers of multi-level marketing in the church (*Consumed by Success* and *All That Glitters Is Not God*) were controversial enough that I didn't even waste my time trying to go the royalty route.

Other examples include John Paulk's book, *Not Afraid to Change: The Remarkable Story of How One Man Overcame Homosexuality.* While a successful agent tried for a full year to sell his manuscript to Christian publishing houses, it was obvious that the topic was too controversial for the mainstream Christian publishing industry. The story of John's high-profile life as a drag-queen before his radical conversion, deliverance, and marriage to a former lesbian was a little too colorful for most. John's commitment to the message of hope for those trapped in the homosexual lifestyle enabled him to take the self-publishing step of faith.

WinePress published 3,000 hardcover copies and when sales took off, reprinted 10,000 softcover copies. Not long after that, John went to work for Focus on the Family and the door was opened—partly due to the success of *Not Afraid to Change*—for Tyndale House to contract him for *Love Won Out,* a story about John and his wife.

In 1998 WinePress published Timothy Williams' book, *The Essential Piece: Living Out Luke 14:26 in Everyday Life.* The book addressed a scripture that many have avoided or simply watered down, where Jesus says:

> If anyone comes to me and does not hate his father and mother, his wife and children, his brothers and sisters—yes, even his own life—he cannot be my disciple. And anyone who does not carry his cross and follow me cannot be my disciple.

Although the obvious intent is not worldly hate, the topic in itself is controversial enough that no royalty publisher would risk their reputation to publish it. But because the underlying foundation was the full message of the Cross—much like the Andrew Murray, A.W. Tozer, William Law, Corrie ten Boom, Francois Fenelon, Amy Carmichael, and Thomas à Kempis books of long ago—WinePress was willing to help Timothy and his wife get the message into print.

Since that book was published in 1999, the entire Williams family has become intimately involved in the framework of WinePress Publishing Group. Timothy Williams, now retired from pulpit ministry, serves as our Executive Publisher; his wife, Carla, is our Editorial & Publicity Director; one son is our Art Director; another, our Multi-Media Director, and another, the author of our theme song, *Winepress of Words*. It has been amazing to watch God provide a family of dedicated Christians to help manage the explosive growth of WinePress and take it to the next level of effectiveness and integrity.

In *Is There a Book Inside You?* Dan Poynter and Mindy Bingham offer a simple quiz to help you determine the best route for your project. I encourage you to prayerfully work your way through this quiz, asking the Lord to confirm the direction you should take.

Publishing Options

Consider the following statements to help decide which publishing option is best for you.

Conventional Publisher

If you feel:

1. It is important to me to be published by a major publisher because I value the type of recognition that would bring.

2. I have a personal connection with a publisher. I know an editor and can get my manuscript considered.

3. Publishers and their editors will change my manuscript for the better. I trust their judgment.

4. I will be happy to accept a 10 percent royalty.

5. Rejection does not bother me. I will keep sending out my manuscript until I find the right publisher.

Then start trying to find a conventional publisher.

Vanity Press

If you feel:

1. I want a few copies of my book for family and friends. It does not have to sell.

2. I am not concerned about price or about getting a return on my investment.

3. I do not want to produce my own book.

Then a vanity press might serve your purposes well.

Book Producer or Packager

If you feel:

1. I want an attractive, professional-looking book.

2. I want someone else to handle the details, to take my manuscript and deliver the books to me to sell.

A book producer might be your answer.

Agent

If you feel:

1. I do not have the time to find a publisher.

2. I would rather create than sell.

3. I am confident of my talent as a writer.

You should try to find an agent.

Self-Publishing

If you feel:

1. I am businesslike as well as creative.

2. I can afford to invest in a business.

3. I want to maintain complete control over my book.

4. If I wait much longer, someone else will beat me to the market.

5. I want a business of my own, and I am willing to put in the time and effort necessary.

6. I want to maximize the return on my efforts.

Self-publishing might be the route for you.[19]

You may have prayerfully determined that self-publishing is the most viable option for your project. But before we move on, let's have a heart-to-heart about what you really need to successfully self-publish and why. The attitude and heart with which you proceed will largely determine the result of your publishing experience, and there's already too much hype out there. I want to give it to you straight.

CHAPTER 2

A Self-Publishing Attitude Adjustment

YOU WANT THE truth? Publishing and promoting a book is hard work and serious business. Some self-publishing companies want you to believe it's glamorous, exciting, quick, easy, and fun. If you truly want to be prepared for the road ahead, you're probably going to need a reality adjustment. So here goes. With the advent of print-on-demand, anybody—and I mean *anybody*—can be an author. Many people who have no business being published are getting their books into print, and that troubles me. It makes it harder for legitimate authors to publish with credibility and even more difficult to stand out from the crowd.

These days, for next to nothing, you can upload an unedited Word document, pick a template cover and voilà . . . you're published. But think about it.

- Is your book meeting a need?
- Has the content received the kind of scrutiny it needs and the level of polishing it requires?

Sure, you can go to your local copy shop or to a "do-it-yourself" self-publisher. If your book is intended only for your family to read and was not written with the hope of reaching people you don't know, doing it yourself not a bad choice. But if God has given you a passion for your message and you want to get that message into the hands of those who need to read it, cutting corners and pinching pennies at the expense of producing a quality product does not glorify God. You need a partner to walk you through the publishing process—a professional team to support you with expert advice.

At WinePress Publishing, we use our experience in the industry to help you develop your message into a professional product. You can't tell the difference between our books and those from Zondervan or Thomas Nelson. Instead, we guide you to do what is best for your manuscript. We help you avoid the mistakes that can steal your credibility. For example:

- Your work may need special attention to obtain permissions for quotes and citations.

- Legal issues may need to be addressed.

- Your cover ideas may be flawed, and if allowed to go to press without feedback, could ruin the future of your message.

- Your title and sub-title may need re-thinking.

- You may have content problems about which you're unaware. Virtually every manuscript we receive needs a professional edit. We take the time to educate our authors so they understand and are motivated to get the level of edit their manuscript needs.

At WinePress, our authors are important to us. When we partner with you, our goal is to make the publishing process an enjoyable journey with the personal touch. You won't get the cookie cutter process with us. We know each book is unique and needs to be treated as such. We're not a one-size-fits-all publisher, quoting stock prices for manuscripts before we've reviewed them. We are a *custom* publisher, and we treat each manuscript with the utmost care. From production to publicity and promotion, we motivate you to run the race that is before you, to persevere and do the hard things that can have eternal consequences.

We don't just get you into print, either; we help you promote and market your book. Our well-rounded publishing and promotions menu includes services no other self-publisher offers, and services most royalty publishers don't offer, such as:

- A full-service in-house publicity department

- Advertising agency services, including copywriting, design, and ad placement in regional or national publications

- Inroads into chain stores such as Parable, Lifeway, Family, Munce, Mardell, Barnes & Noble, etc.

- An audio-visual/multi-media department that's on the cutting edge of technology

- Web site design, hosting and online advertising/marketing campaigns

- Promotional products and programs, author or ministry branding, and customized marketing materials through our sister company, Notation Printing and Marketing Group
- Trade show representation and networking opportunities

It's easy to gravitate towards special offers that hype outdated methods of book promotion. For example, I regularly receive e-mails that promote books. The market is glutted with promotional e-mails, and most people who receive them simply click the *delete* button.

Rather than charging you several hundred dollars to promote your book via e-mail, we offer a cutting edge service whereby we help you strategize how to use your e-mail list effectively. We assign you a personal campaign manager who helps you build your list, weeds out bad e-mails, etc. This program offers quality design for your e-mails, extensive reporting and flexible options.

Well-established in the industry since 1991, we are straightforward and honest with potential authors. Our goal is to meet and exceed your expectations and to serve you with our greatest assets...our team, our expertise and our reputation and connections. Since our solutions advisors are not paid on commission, they are able to offer our authors the best advice and recommendations available. And since we offer both offset and digital (print-on-demand) printing, we are able to help chart the best course for each individual author.

We avoid overpromising or under delivering, so we provide a realistic cost and time-frame for an excellent product. Many POD publishers charge a low start-up fee and then force you to buy 500 copies of your book in order to get a decent discount. We give the highest author discounts in the self-publishing industry (from 50-62 percent), no matter how many copies you order. Our proprietary software allows authors to monitor the production of their book, their sales, and communicate with our staff in an effective and efficient manner.

Countless voices will tell you what you *want* to hear . . . we tell you what you *need* to hear. We want your finished product to receive the "oohs" and "aahs" it deserves.

Another part of your attitude adjustment involves considering whether you should work with a Christian publisher or a secular (general market) publisher. General market publishers have figured out that Christians have something to say, and they are doing their best to capture their fair share of the market.

I'm sure they believe they are offering Christian writers a wonderful opportunity. But if you take a closer look at general market publishers, you'll notice some distinct differences:

1. Christian publishers are much more selective about what they publish. Secular publishers don't have a problem publishing books about topics Christians find offensive, (2 Corinthians 6:14). People will judge your book based on the other books your publisher promotes. Do you feel comfortable being affiliated with them?

2. Our Editorial Director takes great pains to handpick the best editors in Christian publishing—those who hold a Christian world view and do not compromise. I cannot imagine entrusting my work to someone who does not have a personal relationship with Jesus. How could I possibly expect them to critique the content and style of my message with human wisdom alone? (1 Corinthians 2:13). Would you want an unbeliever editing your manuscript?

3. Christian publishers produce products with redemptive value that can be trusted by Christian bookstore buyers. The secular publishers who promote to Christians don't admit that their books are not available through Christian distributors. This is a great disadvantage for a Christian author who seeks to place his or her book in Christian stores. Christian stores do not buy from secular distributors, as there is no filter in place to keep new age and other heresies out. That's why Christian publishers are represented by Christian distributors, and they are the only ones Christian bookstores look to for product. (1 Corinthians 4:2)

4. Christian publishers promote your book in a way that glorifies God, not in a worldly way. We are to be in the world, not of it. How much more so in the way we are represented to the media and the public? (2 Corinthians 1:12)

5. Our Executive Publisher often says, "Above all else, the purpose of WinePress is to glorify God. You'll find this reflected in everything we do, and that is what really makes us different." There is truly no comparison between this purpose and a secular goal to be successful in the business of publishing. (2 Thessalonians 1:12).

It's important to be playing for the same Coach . . . if you're going to get your heart out there to reach people, make sure that the team who helps you cross the finish line has the same goals in mind as you.

At WinePress, we give you the guidance and the tools and the representation . . . we offer you the expertise and the credibility you need. In fact, that's why so many of our WinePress authors are offered contracts from royalty publishing houses. We showcase you to editors and agents because we've helped you make your book the best it can be. Because of our connections, *you* benefit.

Now, I'll share a fraction of the many self-publishing disasters and successes I've experienced first hand over the last few decades.

CHAPTER 3

Self-Publishing Disasters and Successes

A S I SPEAK about self-publishing at Christian writers' conferences, I am amazed at the awful stories I hear. At every stop someone has a tale about their personal publishing nightmare. It seems that those who have been given a message from the Lord and are passionate about blessing others through the written word can be naive regarding the publishing industry and how things work.

If you are considering spending your hard-earned money to self-publish your book, then God expects you to be a good steward of your financial resources. Rather than publishing with the first company that comes along with a great offer, do your homework. Search online for happy and unhappy authors. The more homework you do, the more you will find the WinePress good reputation everywhere. Learn about the different types of self-publishers so you can discern what's right for you and your manuscript.

Subsidy Publishing

In subsidy publishing the author pays for publishing his or her own book, and often at exorbitant prices. This is especially true for print runs of 1,000 copies. In comparison, the price per book for 5,000 copies looks pretty good to the unsuspecting Christian writer.

One company I know of posted a hefty charge per copy for 1,000 copies of a 144-page book, and then touted how much less it would cost per book to print 5,000 copies. The company did not offer any options in between 1,000 and 5,000 quantities, so the only way authors could get a decent price per copy was to publish 5,000 copies.

Does a new author really need 5,000 copies? Usually not, unless the author is in ministry or does a lot of public speaking. This kind of sales technique happens frequently in the self-publishing industry and it is not a benefit to the author. There are, however, times when it does make sense for an author to start off with 5,000 copies rather than 2,500, but that decision must be made with much prayer and consideration, and well informed recommendations from our staff.

Many years ago, before WinePress had distribution and marketing capabilities, a pastor who had been considering our services decided to go to another company that promised to list his book in their catalog. The last time I saw him he hung his head sheepishly as he admitted to sending this "Christian" company $9,000. Six months after he sent the money he had not heard one word from them, but his check had been cashed.

Another acquaintance, a retired pastor, was promised catalog space with a subsidy publisher. Based on their assurance of great sales, he paid close to $20,000 for 5,000 copies of his book. He was a retired pastor! He was not doing any speaking or ministry that would get him in front of prospective buyers. This pastor still has a garage full of books and is desperately doing all he can to get media exposure in order to sell them.

Yet another horror story of unrealized expectations involves Joyce, a woman I met at a Christian writers' workshop. She told me that she found a subsidy publisher in the Christian Writers' Market Guide. They initially quoted her a reasonable price to publish her book, but in the end she paid $5,000 for 400 copies. The cover was ugly, the spine was crooked, it had no ISBN (International Standard Book Number) that all reputable publishers assign to every book, and quite frankly, it looked like it had been assembled by amateurs in a garage.

That same subsidy publisher published four books for Brenda Robinson (a women's ministry leader, speaker, and author from the Atlanta area). As she was working with this publisher on book number five, she was informed—only a few weeks from the time she needed books in her hands—that they could not print a hardcover 6 x 9 book. The publisher insinuated Brenda didn't know what she was doing by requesting that trim size in hardcover and insulted her by saying that she should know better. Brenda called WinePress for help. In no time flat, we gave her a bid for a 6 x 9 hardcover book, exactly the way she wanted it. When the book was published by WinePress she couldn't hold back the tears . . . finally, a REAL book!

On the next page you will see a few examples of the difference between the other publisher's final product and what WinePress created. We have since repackaged all of Brenda's books. Her attractive books give her the credibility she and her message deserve.

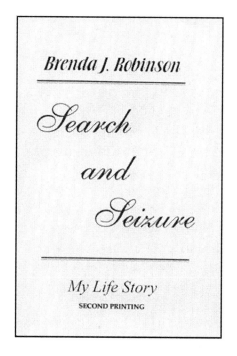

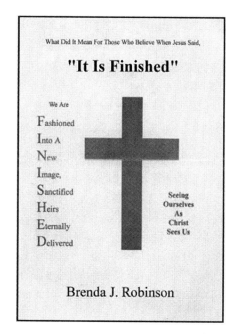

Non-reputable subsidy publisher

WinePress version

While at a writers' conference in Orlando, Florida, I met with another retired minister. He was so excited about the letter he had received from a vanity publisher (who was masquerading as a royalty publisher). The editor told him what a wonderful manuscript he had and assured him it needed to be published. They included a contract to publish 1,000 copies of his book for $14,000! Of course, they offered to market it. But after taking his money up front I doubt they would have any incentive for making a significant marketing effort. Even after paying the $14,000, he still didn't own the books, which is why vanity publishers have such a bad reputation. He only owned the right to 40 percent royalties of the books that might or might not be sold!

At another conference, I met a wonderful man from Ethiopia. He had been in the United States five years and was in full-time ministry. He told me how he had responded to a secular vanity press advertisement in a Christian publication. At the time that I spoke with him, he had spent $18,000 for 3,000 books. The cover was unprofessional at best, and he had to purchase from the publisher any copies he wanted to own or sell. When the book didn't sell during the first year, the vanity press destroyed the inventory after offering him a chance to buy back his books for another $6,000.

I have a friend who ghostwrites for people in ministry who don't have the time or expertise to write their own book. The ghostwriter worked with a pastor who paid a cooperative publishing group $30,000 to print 10,000 copies of his book. The publisher changed the Scripture references from the King James Version to another translation without the author's approval. After pulling the job because he felt they were not acting ethically, the author sued the company in an attempt to get his money refunded.

At WinePress, we hear countless stories of people who pay too much money for an inferior product and, as a result, have a garage full of books. In this thriving industry we continually see new twists on the same old schemes.

In the years since the first edition of *You Can Do It!* was released, I've seen small self-publishing houses start up across the country. Unfortunately, the products from many of these endeavors are sorely lacking in quality control. I've noticed typos on the covers, typos throughout the text, and amateurish formatting and covers. Many of these books receive no marketing or distribution. For this reason, I recommend that you work with a reputable, full service book packager such as WinePress Publishing. This is the only way you will end up with a product you are proud of and that others will take seriously.

In *Advanced Christian Writer,* Sally Stuart, author of the *Christian Writers' Market Guide,* wrote:

> In the past, I have talked about the change of attitude toward self-published or print-on-demand books within the Christian publishing industry . . . While it is true these options are making it possible for more writers to get their books published,

that opportunity also brings with it a responsibility to maintain an appropriate level of professionalism.

Although the stigma attached to self-published books is blurring, it is still true that in order for such a book to get equal attention it must also maintain the highest quality of workmanship. For that reason, you must make every effort to produce a product that is equivalent to a royalty-published book.

Doing so means you must pay someone to design an appropriate cover; use quality paper and a reputable printer; and especially pay a well-qualified editor to do a thorough, line-by-line editing of the manuscript. To take shortcuts in any of these areas will lessen your chances of being noticed—and your book bought—once you get to the marketplace. Ultimately it may also mean that you need to take a realistic look at your project and determine first if you have enough experience and credits to justify producing a book at this point—and then to be sure there is a place and need for it in the market at this time.[20]

Print-on-Demand

With the recent developments in the area of print-on-demand (POD) many new companies that offer publishing "at a fraction of the cost" have sprung up. The disasters I have heard regarding this kind of publishing have been just as dramatic. One writer who attended the 2007 Mt. Hermon Christian Writers Conference explained it well:

"You can find any number of companies who will serve you popcorn . . . [they] slap your text inside an unprofessional front and back cover and say, 'Here's your book!' But with WinePress, even their print-on-demand division serves you a five-course meal, offering everything you could possibly need to create a successful book launch."

One pastor from Texas wrote me about his print-on-demand experience, saying:

They offer no support, no encouragement, not even the common courtesy of returning one's phone calls. I had two editors work my book over, but it didn't matter . . . every person who publishes with that company and doesn't clean their manuscript up puts a blemish on my book as well . . . there is no quality control. The ordering process is not simple . . . you usually have to leave messages on machines for author orders and sometimes they get the order and sometimes they don't. Orders may take two weeks or six, one never knows! . . . I have received three faulty books so far. One I opened with my book cover on it had someone else's book inside! The title page read *My Big Fat Head by Jodie Something.*

In a recent edition of *Advanced Christian Writer*, Sally Stuart reported on a similar situation:

An author who recently had a POD book released shared some of the problems she encountered in trying to promote and sell it:

1. She couldn't get information on the publisher's marketing plan, which it said wouldn't kick in until she had done her local marketing.

2. The publisher wouldn't send her books on consignment for a large local book fair.

3. It promised the book would be available through Ingram Book Company, a major distributor, but it isn't there.

4. A local bookstore ordered a dozen copies for a book signing but could only get a 20 percent discount.

5. She was unable to get any copies to send out for reviews, and the publisher would not provide a list of where it was sending review copies.

6. The highest discount available to the author is 30 percent.[21]

Another author lamented over his print-on-demand experience: "As you may know, my secular POD publisher does not send out review copies, press releases, or in any other way plug the book. So I'm left on my own and I need all the help I can get!"

You just can't be too careful when trying to discern what you're really getting. One Christian POD publisher initially looks less expensive than our Pleasant Word option, until you start adding up all the extras you have to pay for.

Do you have to pay extra to have a returnable book, international distribution, and for the first 10 image placements? Do you only get one or two free books? Are you forced to buy a certain number of books every year to keep your book in print? And how about author discounts? How many books do you have to buy to get a 60% discount or more? Does the publisher's bookstore look like a flashing ad to recruit more authors, or does it look like a bona fide bookstore that is trying to sell your books?

These are all important factors to consider when making a decision.

Watch out for so-called "royalty publishers" who are actually print-on-demand publishers with questionable integrity. There seems to be a trend of what I call "imposter" royalty publishers. These companies claim they are mainline royalty publishers, but they ask for an "author participation fee" of nearly $4,000. These publishers make a huge deal of accepting you as an author and signing a contract, yet the contract guarantees nothing more than a print-on-demand book and 25 free copies to the author. They boast that their investment in your project is $16,000-to-$20,000 of their own dollars, but their list of line items is laughably inflated to anyone who knows the publishing business.

These imposter publishers use gimmicks such as: "Once you sell 5,000 copies of your book, we refund your author participation fee!"

In the royalty publishing realm, only 15 percent of published books ever get close to selling 5,000 copies, so, while that *sounds* good, it is really very little risk to the publisher. Many authors find out too late that their book is inadequately edited and minimally marketed, and come to me with hat in hand, wondering if we can help them with their next project.

Some time ago, I wrote the following warning to our WinePress database of Christian writers:

Too Good to Be True?

Have you ever heard an offer and thought, *that's just too good to be true?* Well, it may just be too good. With today's technology and print-on-demand capacities, the publishing industry can offer many options.

One of the most recent choices popping up on the Christian market are companies— usually secular ones—who want to move into the Christian market. They offer to publish first-time authors without the author having to pay production costs. That sounds pretty good, until you read their contract.

When you sign on the dotted line you give away the rights to the work for seven years. That means if a Christian publisher is interested in your published work during that seven years, they will have to "buy out" your contract . . . something most Christian publishers would not even consider.

Another pitfall to these types of companies is that many of them do not offer publicity packages or accept returned books. Realize that bookstores do not like to take books that they cannot possibly return.

So remember, if it sounds too good to be true, chances are, it probably is. When you self-publish with WinePress or Pleasant Word you retain all rights to your book and have the freedom for major publishers to pick up your work without penalty.

Not long after I made this comment, Sally Stuart updated her *Christian Writers' Market Guide* in *The Christian Communicator*:

I continue to get complaints about ***, a POD publisher that is currently trying to pass itself off as a royalty publisher. Apparently a number of unhappy authors are considering a class-action suit against the company to get back the rights to their books and past-due royalties. Complaints against the company include selling books to which it no longer holds the rights, offering only a 30 percent discount to authors, not paying owed royalties, slipshod editing, unreasonably high retail prices on books, and non-responsiveness. Although some authors tell me they have had a good experience with this company, I do get a number of complaints. I cannot currently recommend that you get involved with this company.[22]

WinePress has developed a print-on-demand program for authors who cannot afford to publish at least 1,500 copies, or for those with a market so small that their need is less than 500 copies. We studied the market diligently and created a strategic alliance with the top on-demand printer in the country. We offer quality print-on-demand and the excellent customer service writers have come to expect from WinePress.

We've built in great publicity and promotions options as well as WinePress-quality editing and cover design. We've watched to see where other POD publishers have missed the boat and made sure that our on-demand division, called Pleasant Word, provides the best service, discounts, and royalties offered in this rapidly-growing industry. This new option gives you a better choice of alternatives so that the word inside you can get out to the world!

Successes

In August of 1995 I completed my first manuscript, *Consumed by Success: Reaching the Top and Finding God Wasn't There*. I wrote it in obedience to a message that I felt the Lord had given me. I had a strong desire to expose the plan of the enemy, who keeps Christians so busy chasing the American Dream that they lose the most important thing in life: their first love, Jesus. In the book, I admit how I nearly destroyed my friendships, family, and faith by getting consumed with multilevel marketing. I didn't write the book to make money. To keep my motives right, I designated all my royalties to two different ministries. I wrote it because I had a burning passion inside to see others set free from the unhealthy pursuit of success—just as I had been.

The first printing of my 96-page book was 2,500 copies. I gave away about 700 copies. I did nearly 100 radio and TV interviews during the first five months after the book's release, and appeared on Money Matters with the late Larry Burkett; Prime Time America with Jim Warren, and many other national and regional Christian talk shows. During the interviews, the Lord continued to give me new insights to share. Since most of the shows encouraged telephone calls from the audience, I heard hundreds of stories from others who had been deceived and victimized by the "get-rich-quick" programs that run rampant through our churches. After only a few months, I had enough material for an updated edition.

I knew that if I wanted the book to be a quality work as well as a convicting message for the body of Christ, I would need some help. So I got together with an editor who helped strengthen the weak parts of the book and enhance the rest with additional dialogue and real-life stories. The revised and expanded 192-page edition came out in May 1996. With a new cover and a stronger message than ever, the book continues to touch people.

As we were heading into our second printing, I whined to the Lord, "Why can't we just get a publisher to buy it? Just think what another self-publishing success story would do for WinePress!"

But the Lord made it very clear: Selling the book to a major publisher could mislead many people into assuming that publishing with WinePress meant they would automatically get picked up by a major publisher. He impressed upon my heart that I needed to be faithful to practice what I preached, be an example for others, and have a successful self-published book that stays self-published.

The book went into four printings within 24 months, and *Today's Christian Woman, The Plain Truth,* and other well known magazines published excerpts, giving the message incredible exposure. *The Bookstore Journal* (recently renamed *Retailers+Resources*) ran a book review encouraging all buyers to keep the book in stock. As I continued to be faithful with the message He had given me, God was faithful to open the doors to get the message out.

The account of how the *Living Bible* was published is another amazing story. Back in the early 1960s, Ken Taylor completed his new translation of the Bible. He shopped it around to different publishers and got nothing but rejections. He believed so strongly in the project that he printed 2,000 copies on his own. It wasn't long before Billy Graham obtained a copy and held it up at a crusade. The rest is history! Tyndale House Publishers hit the map in the publishing industry as the result of this self-published book.

Joseph Girzone also had a self-publishing victory. His novel, *Joshua,* was rejected many times. He published it himself and sold 60,000 copies before selling the rights to a major publisher. Since that time he has written a number of successful sequels.

WinePress author Peter Jones turned down an offer from Bethany House to self-publish his book, *Spirit Wars: Pagan Revival in Christian America* with WinePress. After selling over 15,000 copies, Regal bought the rights and re-titled the work, *Pagans in the Pews.*

Another WinePress author—Holly Wagner—had a similar experience. Her book, *Dumb Things She Does . . . Dumb Things He Does* accompanied her when she spoke to women's groups in Australia. Her book was so well received that HarperCollins in Australia bought the rights and published two books from the one: *Dumb Things We Do*, and *She Loves Me, She Loves Me Not*.

Not long afterwards, we highlighted Holly at the Christian booksellers convention, where she made a significant connection. Thomas Nelson bought the U.S. rights to the book and republished it with the title *Dumb Things He Does/Dumb Things She Does: How to Stop Doing the Things that Drive Women/Men Crazy*. Since that time, Holly has signed a multiple-book contract with Thomas Nelson and is being heavily promoted as one of their up-and-coming authors.

WinePress released *When Duty Calls: A Guide to Equip Active Duty, Guard, and Reserve Personnel and Their Loved Ones for Military Separations* in August, 2001. With the aftermath of 9/11 and the deployment of troops to fight terrorism, Carol Vandesteeg's book became an immediate hit. WinePress contracted with the big distributors that sell to the PXs around the world and with wholesalers who sell directly to the Army, Navy, Air Force, Marines, and Coast Guard. Carol sold 5,000 books in less than six months and reprinted another 10,000. Her first check from the WinePress order fulfillment department for first-month sales was over $7,000. In May of 2005, 25,000 copies later, Cook Communications picked up the rights. They re-released the book in the fall of 2006.

One of the most exciting WinePress success stories is Rosey Dow's *Reaping the Whirlwind*. Her historical fiction/murder mystery, which centered around the Scopes Trial, won a Christy Award in 2001, tying for first place in her category with Gilbert Morris. Self-publishing took a giant step forward when her fiction title won a national award alongside traditional publishers like Zondervan, Thomas Nelson, and Broadman & Holman!

WinePress helped Ron Eaker, M.D., publish his *Holy Hormones* manuscript in 1999 and took him to the Christian booksellers convention, where he experienced tremendous success. After fine-tuning a book proposal on weight control, Ron signed a two-book contract in 2006 with Bethany House for a revised edition of *Holy Hormones* and his new book, *Fat Proof Your Family*.

Another exciting success story is Heather Paulsen's book, *Emotional Purity*. WinePress published 2,500 copies, which got a great response at the bookseller's convention. The first printing sold out, and Heather reprinted 10,000 copies. Partway through the sales of the second print run, Crossway Books picked up the rights and re-released it in April of 2007.

This year, after one print run of 5,000 copies and a reprint of 2,500 copies, Dorothy Valcarcel's book *The Man Who Loved Women* was sold to Baker Book House. The encouraging part of the story is that Dorothy's agent, Joyce Hart of Hartline Literary Agency, spent a year pitching the book to royalty publishers with no success. She knew it had to get into print, so Joyce sent her to WinePress to help get the message out there. Once Joyce had some sales numbers to take back to the Acquisitions Editor at Baker, she was able to land a contract for Dorothy.

Yet another WinePress success story was shared in a newsletter to our database of writers:

Is the Grass Really Greener?

From Self-Publishing to Traditional . . . and Back Again!

Trying to decide on the best avenue for publishing can be agonizing for authors. With the many options available, how does a person know the publishing choice best for their message? Rebecca Ingram Powell, author of *Baby Boot Camp* (WinePress 2000), offers authors her insights as both a self-published and a traditionally published author who will soon return to WinePress to publish a print-on-demand book through Pleasant Word.

Rebecca printed 5,000 copies of *Baby Boot Camp* in September, 2000. Her first piece of advice to authors is, "You must have a Web site. An author who doesn't have a Web site is like an author who is still using a manual typewriter." After her books arrived, Rebecca immediately realized she needed to regularly publicize her book, so she started a weekly e-mail devotional. Rebecca sent it to everyone she knew and had a place on her Web site for people to sign up. She placed the name of her book and ordering information on every newsletter.

Through a well-known women's ministry, Rebecca developed a speaking ministry. She made herself available to do retreats, Bible studies and whatever doors opened up. She also wrote articles on her topic, placing her credentials and the name of her book in the bio at the end of each article.

Rebecca was fortunate to establish a monthly column with *ParentLife* magazine, which kept her book in the public's eye. She heard that *ParentLife* had just hired a new editor and knew this would be a prime time to approach the magazine with her book and writing samples, adding that "because I had printed with WinePress my book did not look self-published." After purchasing an article from Rebecca, the editor later looked to her to fill a columnist slot that had opened up. Rebecca has been a monthly columnist for *ParentLife* for three years.

As *Baby Boot Camp* began to sell, and she had moved over 2,500 books, Rebecca realized she could now approach a traditional publisher since she had demonstrated a market for her topic. She counsels authors to research the market and find the right publisher.

Blindly peddling proposals to publishers is a waste of both your time and theirs. She began praying that God would lead her to the right publisher. One day she picked up a Bible study book and noticed the publisher New Hope. God clearly spoke to her and told her to contact them. It "so happened" that she had an upcoming speaking engagement in the town where New Hope was located and an editor agreed to meet with her about her book. They offered her a contract and her book has been in print for about a year now!

So how does Rebecca's experience with both self-publishing and traditional publishing compare? She says, "One thing that does not change is that you still have to promote your book. If people aren't willing to publicize their books they shouldn't publish at all. You must believe in your message and know other people can use it. No one will be as passionate about your message as you."

Having experienced both sides of publishing, Rebecca has decided to return to self-publishing with a new project. She emphasized the quality of WinePress products and that our toll-free ordering number gave her credibility when doing media interviews.

"The self-publishing experience taught me so much. I learned how to lean on the Lord in a totally new way and I experienced God afresh as I went out on a limb. WinePress made it easy because the people were so easy to work with and helpful. When I filled out the online form and I got a personal call from Athena, it was so reassuring. There's a trust factor at WinePress."[23]

So, don't always assume that the grass is greener. Custom-publishing through WinePress offers the best of both worlds!

Maggie Kinney of Dallas, Texas, has been helping local authors self-publish for many years. In 1993 her pastor had an idea for a book of quotations about God and America and began putting the information together. She packaged the book for him, and they named it *America's God and Country*. Since that time they have sold more than 100,000 copies. They're not interested in selling it to a publisher—they're doing just fine without one!

Colene Copeland, author of the *Priscilla the Pig* series, cheerfully admits that she's self-published and that after selling nearly 700,000 copies of the first book alone, she remains self-published "to keep more of the money."

Consider the phenomenal story of *The Christmas Box*.

Utah advertising writer Richard Paul Evans originally printed [twenty] copies of his short parable about a parent's love for a child to share with family members. When people around his home began asking local bookstores for it (one bookseller received [ten] orders for it), Evans decided to find a publisher. After repeated rejections ("un-categorizable," "too long," "too short"), he published himself, starting with 3,000 paperback copies distributed mainly in the West. By the time Simon & Schuster bought hardcover rights in a frenzied auction last February, Evans had sold 700,000 copies.[24]

WinePress author Dan Miller, whose inspirational life story *Living, Laughing, and Loving Life!* has sold almost 80,000 copies, has been offered royalty contracts over and over again, but chooses to remain self-published.

Print-on-Demand Successes

A *New York Times* article shared more print-on-demand success stories:

After spending a year trying to sell her book to publishers and receiving 70 rejection letters as a reward, Laurie Notaro, a newspaper columnist in Phoenix, decided to do it herself. Working with [a secular POD publisher], one of many companies that offer "print-on-demand" services . . . several months later she sold the rights to her book, plus the concept for a new one, to a major publisher for a six-figure sum.

Joe Vitale, on the other hand, had already published several business books with traditional publishers. But for a new book, Mr. Vitale, a marketing consultant in Austin, Tex., decided to try another print-on-demand company, ***. For two days in June, Mr. Vitale's book was the bestselling title on Amazon.com.

In the same way that the home computer gave users the ability to create documents that looked good, even if they didn't necessarily read well, print-on-demand services enable people to publish a book with ease, regardless of whether anyone else would want to read it.

For [not much money], such companies offer a professionally laid-out book, a choice of stock or customized covers and an International Standard Book Number, or ISBN, which is used to list the book in databases open to traditional and online bookstores.

For those fees, authors also get up to 10 copies of their book, and can buy additional copies, typically for 60 percent of the retail price. With the print-on-demand model, there is no minimum print run; books do not end up stored in a warehouse and possibly destroyed after a few months' run. Yet they never go out of print; the digital file is stored indefinitely, always available for creating another hardback or paperback book when needed.

"The POD books that succeed are not the best books," said Mr. Feldcamp of [a leading POD publisher]. "They're the ones that have been pushed most successfully by their authors."

As an experienced newspaper columnist, Ms. Notaro knew that traditional marketing techniques would get her nowhere. She did not bother to send her book, a collection of humorous essays called *The Idiot Girls' Action Adventure Club,* to newspapers to be reviewed.

"I knew how the process worked," she said. "My book would fall to the bottom of the pile." She rejected the publisher's stock covers and designed one of her own. Trading on her name recognition in Phoenix, Ms. Notaro organized readings at libraries, schools and women's groups, also handing out fliers telling people to order her book at Amazon.com. Using a now-defunct Amazon.com marketing program, she created a "sponsored link" on the Web site. A literary agent noticed it, contacted her and eventually sold her book to Villard, one of the publishers that had originally rejected it. As a paperback from a mainstream publisher, it made the New York Times bestseller list for several weeks last summer.

Mr. Vitale sent 8,000 e-mail messages asking people to buy his book, *Spiritual Marketing: A Proven Five-Step Formula for Easily Creating Wealth from the Inside Out,* from Amazon.com on one of two specified days last June; in return he offered them access to marketing articles posted at his Web site that normally were not available without a fee. He also recommended his own book on an Amazon.com page featuring a competitor's work.

Mr. Vitale's guerrilla marketing tactics paid off. He sold 5,000 copies on his two requested days, plus an additional 2,500 to date. "I didn't care about getting reviews," he said. "I was easily able to drive people to Amazon.com, and by becoming the best-selling book for two days, I got a lot of attention."

Too often, writers who use print-on-demand services do not put enough energy or money into their efforts, expecting that somehow their work will become known. "People who flock to print-on-demand are very frequently planning to fail," said Richard Galli, a writer. His first book, *Rescuing Jeffrey,* was bought by an established publisher.

For his next book, a novel, Mr. Galli wanted to keep his ownership rights and all the profits, so he chose to use a subsidy press and print thousands of copies at once.[25]

One of our print-on-demand success stories is Claude Hickman. We published his *Live Life on Purpose* project under our Pleasant Word imprint. He already had an established speaking ministry but having a book in print took him to a new level. Using the book as a calling card for his ministry, he presented it to conference planners with different denominations to offer as part of their upcoming youth conferences. While he sold about 800 copies of the print-on-demand version, he took orders for another 5,000 copies to ministries across the country. One denomination bought 4,000 copies to give to each attendee at their annual youth conference, another bought 400, another 300, and so on. The income produced from selling 5,000 copies at a 50 percent discount enabled him to reprint 10,000 copies and still have money left over. In early 2008 he reprinted another 5,000 copies!

Ben Young's *Why Bert's Not a Christian: A Conversation with Skeptics*, is another great story of spring-boarding from print-on-demand to a larger print run and then, to a royalty contract. This well-known youth pastor from the Houston area needed 500 copies in short order for a seasonal event, so he started with Pleasant Word. He then reprinted 2,500 copies of his book with WinePress and had sold nearly all of them when Harvest House Publishers picked up the rights, re-titled the book *Why Mike's Not a Christian: Questions Skeptics are Asking About Faith,* and released it in 2006.

The most recent proof of the viability of self-publishing is the unprecedented success story of *The Shack*. Turned down by virtually every royalty Christian publisher, the author, his editor, and a friend started Windblown Media, and maxed out every possible credit card they had to get the book into print. After selling one million copies in the first two months of publication through a low budget grassroots effort, they signed with Hachette Publishing Group to co-publish and take over responsibilities for sales, marketing, distribution, licensing, and manufacturing.[26]

Other self-publishing successes include *The One-Minute Manager, What Color Is Your Parachute?* and *Managing from the Heart,* plus many secular blockbusters, such as *The Celestine Prophecy, Mutant Message Down Under,* and *Surfing the Himalayas,* and *Rich Dad, Poor Dad.*

It is exciting to see how often our authors are offered contracts by royalty publishers, but it's even more exciting to see authors do so well with us that they turn down contracts offered to them by other publishers, saying, "Why do I need them?"

Regardless of the outcome of your project, the self-publishing experience should be a positive one for you, not a nightmare. Your book may not be picked up by a major publisher, so you still need realistic expectations along with pure heart motives.

CHAPTER 4

What's Your Heart Motive?

· ·

WHY DO YOU write? Have you ever thought about your bottom-line motivations for becoming a published author? Scripture states, "The heart is deceitful above all things, and desperately wicked; who can know it?" (Jer. 17:9). We need to ask the Lord to purify our motives and to warn "if there is any wicked way" in us (Ps. 139:24). If we truly want the Lord to use our writing to minister to others, we must ensure that our writing flows from a clean and pure heart.

Why do you write? Is it for personal enjoyment? Is it to aid in and record your spiritual growth? (Journaling is a good example of this.) Is it to earn part- or full-time income (tentmaking)? Is it to teach or help others? Or is it for ministry purposes? Once you establish your reason for writing, ask the Lord to purify your motives.

No matter what we do in life, it is motivated by one of two things: God or self. When our motives truly become selfless instead of selfish, and we seek God's face and hear directly from Him on what we are to write and how we are to write it, we can be sure that the Lord will minister to those who read our work.

Another area that must be checked is the root of our message. Are we telling our story to make a killing (greed)? To set the record straight (anger)? To right a wrong (unforgiveness, bitterness, or revenge)? To see our name in lights (pride and selfish ambition)? Because something terrible may happen if we don't get this word out (fear)?

A woman once asked us to design and publish her book. It had already been mentioned in a denominational magazine as a "must read," and she was adamant that we help her get it into book form. It turned out that the book was an exposé of a denomination's financial mismanagement at their regional headquarters, which resulted in many pastors losing their retirement income after years of faithful service in the ministry. The more I listened to this woman, the more evident it became that her manuscript was written out of revenge and bitterness. She was the wife of one of those pastors and wanted to tell the truth so that the denomination would take responsibility for its sin. Even though she had money in hand and wanted WinePress to publish her book, I knew that God would not honor that message if it was written from a root of bitterness. We chose not to co-labor in that particular project since it would have given God's work a "black eye." Even though we could have used the money at the time, I knew the Lord would bring other jobs to meet our obligations.

Sometimes I meet people in the Christian publishing world who turn their noses up at self-publishing. They say: "I would never consider spending my own money to print my books. I wouldn't lower myself to that." I see pride written all over their faces and am saddened that confessing Christians could be so full of self.

It's also easy to fall into prideful thinking when we become convinced that our manuscript came from God word-for-word and it doesn't need any editing. Sometimes I want to ask, "If the God who dictated your book is the same God of the universe who created all things, then how come He doesn't know how to spell? Certainly God has better grammar than that!"

We need to be willing to be teachable and to take honest criticism so our work becomes the best it can be for God. Joining a Christian writers' critique group may be the first step in crucifying the flesh, dealing a death blow to our pride, and holding ourselves accountable to others who are going in the same direction with their writing.

In 1995, while I was teaching at Seattle Pacific University's writers' conference,* I heard a creative song with a lot of truth. It was written by two attendees, and they've given me permission to share the lyrics.

If I Were An Author

© 1995 by Margaret D. Smith and Janet Lee Carey

(To the tune of "If I Were A Rich Man")

If I were an author
Diga-diga-diga-diga-diga-deeze.
All day long I'd fax a little book,
Keep Oprah on hold,
Stacking up my royalties.

*The SPU conference is now produced by Northwest Christian Writers' Association and is a great conference to attend. See more info at www.nwchristianwriters.org.

What's Your Heart Motive?

I wouldn't have to work hard
With my staff of twelve to handle all my
photographic crew.
All day long I'd think immortal thoughts,
Make up brilliant plots,
With characters too vivid to be true.

Bridge:
I'd call my publishers at home at midnight
Just to chat a little bit.
They'd have to sit and listen to all my dreams.
And when *New Yorker* came to beg forgiveness
For ignoring childhood genius in my poems,
I'd grant them an exclusive interview.
Ya-da-da-dee-da-da
Ya-da-da-dee-da-da
I wouldn't be rejected,
Neener-neener-neener-neener-neener-neener-neener-noo.
Everyone would ask for my next book,
I'd keep them on the hook,
And tell them I had better things to do . . . like . . . Going on vacation
To the south of France or maybe on a little yacht in Spain.
Hey here comes the mailman with my book,
Here, let's take a look . . .
Guess I'll have to send it out again.

Bridge:
Until they finally recognize my potential,
Talent dripping from my every pore,
I'll have to stop this song and write . . .
Some . . . more!

Ya-da-da-da-da-da
Ya-da-da-da-da-da-da-da-da-da-da-da-da-da
Hiya!

This song pokes gentle fun at the vain imaginations of seeing our name in lights. If our motivation is rooted in pride, sooner or later we will be disappointed!

Is your motive to get published, no matter what it takes? To see your name on a book, whatever the cost? To be an author rather than "merely" a writer?

About 15 years ago, when I first started participating on editorial panels at various Christian writers' conferences, I would hear interesting suggestions offered by Christian publishing "experts." Someone in the audience would ask what the represented publishing houses were looking for in the way of publishable material. Inevitably someone on the panel would suggest that the person check out what was selling in the American Booksellers Association (ABA) market, the secular counterpart to the Christian Booksellers Association. Panelists suggested that similar trends would arise in the Christian market and recommended that authors write toward that end. Only in the last five or six years have I begun to hear editors on these panels encourage Christian writers to write from their passion.

Writing may or may not turn out to be a profit-making venture, but for Christians, writing should be a ministry aimed at bringing life to those who read the message. If we are not anointed by the Holy Spirit to write on a subject, then the "wood, hay and stubble" that 1 Corinthians 3:12 speaks about will be the result. Yes, you might be able to sell your manuscript to a publisher, but unless it has come as a result of the passion burning within you, it will fall short of the glory of God. It will be just another book with no anointing—no power through the Holy Spirit to bring change to its readers.

These words may be offensive to some who make their living cranking out books for major Christian publishers, but as industry professional Leonard Goss shared at a writers' conference in Philadelphia:

> . . . in Christian publishing, our sense of business may be taking over our sense of critical [judgment]. Maybe you have heard the phrase, "the publisher's smell." The publisher's smell is what we feel comfortable publishing. I'm afraid that the publisher's smell may be changing—even in Christian publishing. Many in Christian publishing today are unconcerned about the right choice of what to publish. Rather, they are concerned only with sales and with bringing their wares to the market. This is the jackpot syndrome.

> When George Bernard Shaw once said of publishing, "There is probably no other trade where there is so little relationship between profits and actual value or into which chance so largely enters," he had no clue what would become of Christian publishing—but Shaw certainly described Christian publishing. Now the idea is to package the books right so they appeal only to the very general reader representing the blasé Christian mainstream. The idea is simply to publish more books that sell more, and fewer books that have a limited reading audience. The idea is to compete with the electronic media for the entertainment dollar, to bring all the glitz and all the visual appeal to books that one associates with the electronic media.

We need to learn to wait on God, hear His voice, and use the gift of writing in the way He instructs, not just plot what will sell or dream up a good idea or crank out a formula. We must sit at Jesus' feet and let Him refine us, mold us, purify us, and make us a vessel of honor. Then—and only then—can we be effective messengers with the words He gives us.

CHAPTER 5

Industry Terms

· ·

THE VOCABULARY OF the publishing industry may seem like a foreign language when you're starting out. Sometimes I throw around terms, assuming everyone knows what I'm talking about. Thankfully, someone always brings me back down to earth by asking, "What is a subsidy publisher?"

In this chapter, I'll clarify some of the terms mentioned in the first few chapters. As I define each term, I'll give you my take on the pros and cons of each kind of publishing. Most of these definitions are excerpted from Dan Poynter's book, *The Self-Publishing Manual*, but some are my own descriptions.

> THE BIG PUBLISHING FIRMS are like department stores; they have something for everyone. They publish in many different fields and concentrate on books that anticipate audiences in the millions . . . They put up the money, have the book produced, and use sales reps to get it into bookstores, but they will not promote the book. The author must do it . . . They pay you an average of 15 percent on the wholesale price collected for your book . . .[27]

The upside of getting a contract with a publishing firm or "royalty publisher" is:

1. No risk: You put no money up and just go along for the ride.
2. Credibility: Getting a contract with a royalty publisher gives credibility to your message.

3. Almost guaranteed to get your book on the shelves: The reason I say *almost* is because this is still not a guarantee. With shelf space shrinking and celebrity authors increasing, even authors who land a deal with a royalty publisher may not find their book on the shelves of Christian and general market bookstores.

The downside of getting a contract with a big publishing firm is:

1. You have no control. Your book belongs to the publisher and since they are spending their money, they call the shots. Editorial changes and decisions regarding the title and cover are not yours to make. You also have no control over how long your book stays in print.

2. Since you are not risking your money on the project, you receive only a small royalty instead of the profits from the sales. A normal royalty for a first-time author is between 10 and 15 percent but that percentage is of the net, not the retail price of your book. If your book retails for $12.00, your royalty would run anywhere from about 50 cents to one dollar per book. You would also have the opportunity to buy your book from the publisher at a discount usually ranging from 40 percent to 60 percent (somewhere between $5 to $7.50 per book), and sell those books for $12.00. To illustrate the magnitude of this point, I'll share a story of the first book I worked on back in 1988. It was a ministry project and because the executive director of the ministry was not well known, no publisher was willing to offer a contract. The ministry finally found someone in the business who knew how to edit, typeset, do cover design, and establish an ISBN number, bar code, etc. The ministry paid $11,000 for 10,000 copies of this 144-page book (that was before the paper prices skyrocketed in the early 90s), and sold them all in two years. Many of them sold for a 50 percent discount, and the ministry gave at least 2,000 copies away. From those 10,000 copies (8,000 actually sold), the ministry made over $40,000 in profits. Multnomah Press bought the rights to the book in 1990 and sold almost 40,000 copies over the next nine years. Between the 15 percent royalty they paid the author and the copies the ministry bought back from the publisher to resell at events, the ministry only made $21,000 on those 40,000 copies . . . that's right: $21,000 on 40,000 copies compared to $40,000 on 8,000 copies!

3. It is difficult to get a contract with a royalty publisher. As we discussed earlier, the likelihood of getting published if you aren't a big name is slim to none.

4. It is difficult to get your book placed on the shelf in a Christian bookstore. A book buyer from a local Family Christian Store told me that only 15–20 percent of their sales volume comes from books.

5. You are expected to bring a lot "to the (negotiating) table." Many publishers expect to see a 50–60 page book proposal where you not only critique your competition and show how your project differs but also commit to spending your hard-earned advance to purchase outside publicity services or to buy back copies of your book to do special promotions. Whether your platform is a speaking ministry or hosting a daily or weekly TV or radio show, publishers are looking for situations that require much less risk on their part and result in much larger sales potential.

> VANITY OR SUBSIDY PUBLISHERS [also called contract publishing] offer regular publishing services, but the author invests the money . . . ($10,000 to $30,000). [Authors receive 40 percent of the retail price of the books sold.] . . . Subsidy publishers don't make any promises regarding sales and usually the book sells fewer than 100 copies. The vanity publisher doesn't have to sell any books because the author has already paid him for his work . . . Since binding is expensive, the subsidy publisher often binds a few hundred copies; the rest of the sheets remain unbound unless needed. The "advertising" promised in the contract normally turns out to be only a "tombstone" ad listing many titles in the New York Times.[28]

The only upside for this kind of publishing is:

1. You'll get your book into print.

I could go on for pages about the downside of subsidy publishing, but I'll just list the most obvious cons:

1. You pay big money but you don't own your books. You pay an enormous sum for publishing services and you are paid a royalty from the books that sell. If you want copies you have to buy them at a set cost, and if they don't sell fast enough, the publisher has the right to destroy the inventory.
2. Unprofessional product. Most vanity publishers have no concern whether you ever sell copies of your book, so they don't care whether your book looks good. The covers are unattractive, text is squeezed onto the page in a way that makes it hard on your eyes to read, and the editorial work is sloppy, at best.
3. No credibility in the bookstore market. Bookstores are aware of "vanity presses" and won't carry their product. If your book doesn't look like a book produced by a royalty publisher, your chances of getting it onto the shelves of a bookstore are virtually non-existent.

BOOK PACKAGERS are graphic arts shops that specialize in the production of books. They will edit the manuscript, design the book, set the type and lay out the pages. When the book is printed, it is delivered to you. Book packagers (or producers) do not invest in books, they do not promote books, and they do not store or ship books. They only put them together . . .[29]

The upside to using a book packager, which is what we used on that first book I worked on in 1988, is:

1. You'll get a professional product. As long as the company has a reputation of working with many authors and producing quality products, you'll end up with a book you're proud of.

The downside to using a book packager is:

1. No distribution. Book packagers don't connect you with distributors or offer any help in making those necessary contacts and agreements. The books come to you and you must figure out how to get them out to the readers. It is important to understand that book buyers are not interested in buying books from authors or really even from the publisher. They want to go to one source and get all the books they need for their store. The only way for them to do that is to buy from a distributor. A distributor carries titles from hundreds of publishers and can fill 99 percent of all the requests the same day the order is placed.

2. No promotional or marketing help. Book packagers will not help get your book noticed by the media; they don't help you schedule radio or TV interviews or get reviews in local papers or magazines. Neither do they make your book available for sale at online stores. Finally, book packagers do not promote your book to the Christian bookstore market.

3. You're on your own once the book packaging is completed. Many authors don't realize that the real work begins after their book rolls off the press. That's when you need support and guidance—an advocate who represents you to the media and trade.

4. It's almost impossible to get your book on the shelves of the bookstores or even available through them. Again, because you have no established distribution system or publisher backing you, you'll receive no exposure to the bookstore market.

Industry Terms

LITERARY AGENTS match manuscripts with the right publisher and negotiate the contract; most new material comes to publishers through agents. The agent has to serve the publisher well; if he or she submits an inappropriate or poor manuscript, the publisher will never offer another appointment. Therefore, agents like sure bets, too, and many are reluctant to even consider an unpublished writer. Their normal commission is 15 percent . . .

According to *Literary Agent's Marketplace*:

- 40 percent of the book agents will not read manuscripts by unpublished authors
- 15 percent will not even answer query letters from them

Of those agents who will read the manuscript of an unpublished author:

- 80 percent will charge for the service, but...
- 80 percent of the agents will not represent professional books
- 93 percent will not touch reference works
- 99 percent will not handle technical books
- 98 percent will not represent regional books, satire, musicals and other specialized manuscripts
- 20 percent are willing to take on either novelettes or short stories
- 2 percent have a special interest in literature or quality fiction

On the fringe, there are several "agents" who charge a "reading fee," and then pay students to read and critique the manuscript. They make their money on the fees, not from placing the manuscripts.[30]

The upside to having an agent is:

1. An agent has a better chance than you do to land you a contract with a royalty publisher.
2. An agent lends credibility to your writing and message.

The downside to having an agent is:

1. An agent is not so easy to get. Most credible agents don't take on an author unless the author is highly marketable to the publisher. The writing must be incredibly good, the author must have a platform (such as a speaking ministry) from which to sell thousands of books, and the author must be able to crank out more than one book.

2. The author gives away 15 percent of the book's royalties to the agent.

> SELF-PUBLISHING is where the author by-passes all the middlemen, deals directly with the printer and then handles the marketing and distribution. If you publish yourself, you will make more money, get to press sooner and keep control of your book. You will invest your time as well as your money, but the reward is greater; you will get it all.[31]

The statement "you will get it all" is true only if you choose the right printer and know how to market and promote your book. The statement is true if you don't spend too much money on the wrong advertising, or if you don't print more books than you could ever sell.

Many books about self-publishing, marketing, and distribution are geared to the general market. If you try to market and distribute a Christian book through secular channels, you will waste valuable time and money.

The upside to self-publishing is:

1. You have complete control. You call the shots regarding the editing, the formatting, the cover, the quantity, and the overall production of the product.
2. Self-publishing is your most cost-effective option . . . *if you avoid making costly mistakes* (we'll talk more about that in a minute).

The downside to self-publishing is:

1. You are fully responsible for the product you end up with.
2. You might make very expensive mistakes. I can't tell you how many times authors have told us that God has shown them what needs to be on their book's cover, or that they know exactly what the perfect cover should look like. One example is Donna Fitzpatrick's *Learning to Hear the Whispers of God*. She was sure the cover needed to be black and white, the white representing God's voice coming through the darkness. I cringed when I heard that, knowing Donna's cover design could never compete at the Christian booksellers convention (now known as the International Christian Retail Show) or in bookstores. Even though Donna thought she knew what she wanted, I asked our designer to come up with another option, and encouraged him to be creative. The cover he designed was so beautiful (see sample) the author gasped when she saw it. There was no question in Donna's

mind as to which cover was the right choice. If you self-publish on your own, there is no one to stop you from doing what you "think" is right, or what you "feel" is God's will. Donna may have paid more for our services at WinePress than if she had done it all on her own . . . but she's glad she did. She would have wasted all the money she thought she was saving by self-publishing a book with a black and white cover.

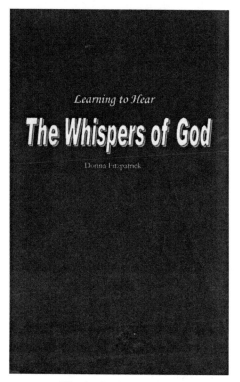

The Author's Design

Our Design

Here's another example of a potentially expensive self-publishing blunder: When Eddie Spencer set out to publish his second book, he had someone design his cover and thought it would work just fine. He asked us to publish his book and showed us the cover design. The minute I viewed the cover, I knew we would not be doing him justice by allowing that cover on his book. I asked if we could give him another option for the cover and re-title the book. The initial title was *Controlling Your Anger Before It Destroys You, Your Family and Your Future.* That sounded like a long subtitle, not a title. When our editorial director and I brainstormed titles, Carla suggested, *Put Out the Fire.* We tweaked the subtitle down to: "How to Control Your Anger Before it Destroys Your Life." The art director came up with a great concept, and as you can see below, the difference is quite literally night and day.

Before

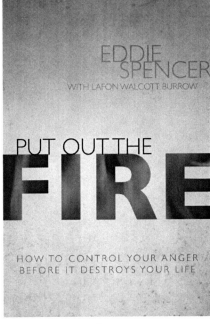

After

3. You're totally on your own. You have to figure out how to distribute your book, how to fill orders, how to handle bad checks and credit card declines. In order to promote your book, you've got to go to the media and ask for interviews. When you self-publish on your own, you have no one to be your advocate or to represent you.

4. You have to know where to find a good editor. I've had many people tell me that their high school teacher edited their book, so they don't need any editing. The book publishing industry abides by the standards in *The Chicago Manual of Style, Fifteenth Edition*. This is not the book most English teachers were trained with. If your book is not edited by a professional editor, you are shortchanging yourself and your message.

5. You have to know how to design and format your book or find someone who does. The catch is, with the popularity of desktop publishing, everyone and their brother "knows how to" design and format a book. I've seen a lot of hokey-looking books formatted by someone claiming to be a professional. One of our authors

paid $3,500 to a "professional" who typeset his 600-page book in 14-point Arial (that's very unprofessional), with separate, unlinked text blocks on every page. When we repackaged his book, we had to undo everything he had paid for since it was done incorrectly. The author wanted to add a paragraph on page 29, but since the text did not flow throughout the document, the manuscript would not repaginate.

6. Self-published books, when not packaged by a professional, are often missing the bar code or other industry standards. Most distributors will not carry such books, since lack of a bar code makes it difficult for bookstores to find the books so they can special order them, let alone put them on the shelves. I have been the special order person for our local bookstore and customers regularly request titles I'm not familiar with. When I search for the requested title, I first check with the distributor from whom I order regularly (Spring Arbor Distributors, a division of Ingram Distributors). Spring Arbor carries over 50,000 titles; if I can't find a product there, I'll check with STL Distributors, and if it's not there, I'll try the publisher. Most special order people won't try that hard. If a title is not available from their regular distributor, they won't bother to try to find it.

New Alternatives

Today's technology offers many new options for getting your book into print; from e-books to Web publishing to print-on-demand; these options make your book accessible. Of these alternatives to traditional publishing, the print-on-demand option lands at the top of the list for small-quantity runs. Unlike Web publishing and e-books, POD gives the reader a book to curl up with.

Print-on-Demand: A company takes self-edited, camera-ready copy and typically designs a plain cover and prints from one to 250 copies of the book. The publisher makes the book available to the author at a small discount, as well as to traditional and online bookstores. The author is paid a small royalty when the publisher sells the book via the Web, via an online bookstore, or via brick-and-mortar bookstores.

The upside to POD publishing is:

1. Much smaller cash outlay
2. Cost-effective, if you anticipate selling 500 or fewer copies.
3. Fast turn-around for both your initial printing and reprints.

The downside to POD publishing is:

1. Over time you pay more. If you sell close to 2,500 books, you actually pay more with POD publishing.
2. Many bookstores have been disgusted with POD-published books. Some companies' POD books are not returnable. Bookstores are leery of buying books that don't have a guaranteed return policy.
3. Questionable quality. While some POD printers are better than others, this technology offers limited options for trim sizes and paper choices. And POD book covers use only high-gloss lamination, rather than matte lamination or embossing.
4. Little, if any, quality control. Most POD publishers take the text you give them and put it into book format using Times New Roman font and Microsoft Word (very unprofessional). Your book could be featured on their bookstore or in their catalog next to another book that is filled with typos and has an ugly cover. Let's face it; you are judged by those with whom you are associated.

While print-on-demand technology continues to evolve, up until recently it has remained somewhat deficient in quality control. If you're looking into print-on-demand, follow this rule of thumb: if the prices for on-demand are low, quality control is either non-existent or sorely lacking.

It took WinePress a good five years of waiting and watching before we felt comfortable creating a partnership with a digital printer. In 2002, when we established Pleasant Word, we partnered with the leader in on-demand printing. We feel great about what we are able to offer in this arena, presenting the same high-quality services that the industry has come to expect from WinePress. In fact, the book you hold in your hands right now was produced using on-demand printing technology.

Print-on-demand poses still other limitations, such as the inability to offer high-end cover embellishments (embossing, matte, spot gloss lamination, or foil stamping), special bindings such as lay-flat (Otabind) binding, spiral binding, or French flaps, and page counts fewer than forty-eight, as well as limitations in publicity options. But if those limitations don't pose a problem, then POD can be a great way to test-market your project! *See chapter 6 for more detail on the upside and downside of a large print run vs. print-on-demand.

E-Books—Online Publishing: The author submits a manuscript to an online publisher and an e-book is created in a format that may be downloaded by customers. The company typically creates a cover, but does not edit your work. The author is paid a royalty for any copies that are downloaded off the publisher's Internet site.

The upside to E-books/online publishing is:

1. Minimal or no cash outlay.
2. Some companies operate like traditional publishers and won't accept just anybody.

The downside to E-books/online publishing is:

1. Most people won't bother to print out a large manuscript on their printer.
2. E-books are available but the concept hasn't really caught on. *Publishers Weekly* notes, "Despite the fast growth, e-books will still make up a tiny share of the market—no more than 2 percent of sales for most titles—and will contribute only a minimal amount to publishers' bottom lines."[32]
3. Most people don't like reading an entire book on the computer screen since it's hard on the eyes.
4. You can't curl up in bed with your computer . . . unless, of course, it's a laptop, a Pocket PC, or an e-book reader. And electronic reading devices are not catching on the way industry experts had hoped. The February 2008 issue of *Consumer Reports* says, "Although the new Kindle and revamped Sony Reader should suit voracious readers on the go, most people still want to stick with paper."[33]

Cooperative Publishing: A royalty publisher agrees to publish your book but requires you to collaborate in several specific ways.

> You, as the author, commit to purchasing half of the 5,000 print run at a 43 [percent] discount off the assessed retail price of the book. The publisher retains the other half of the print run in [a] warehouse for distribution. The author is paid a quarterly royalty on the sale of those books. The royalty percentage is determined before contract signing. The publisher uses all its resources to produce a high-quality book. The author is required to do everything possible to help market and publicize the book, being available for radio and television interviews the publisher may choose to schedule.[34]

Another company out there who offers a cooperative publishing contract requires the purchase of at least 1,000 copies at such a low discount (20% off the retail price) that you're practically forced to buy 5,000 copies to get a decent discount. I've met many authors who were disappointed with the actual marketing they received compared to the promises they were made by this well-known publisher.

The upside to cooperative publishing is:

1. The publisher promotes at their own expense.

The downside to cooperative publishing is:

1. Unfulfilled marketing promises. One author asked a cooperative publisher for some satisfied authors to check with before signing a contract. They refused. He did his homework and contacted five authors who had published with this company. They were all disappointed with the follow-through on the marketing and promotion promises the company agreed to.

   Another author who published with a cooperative company said it took three years to get her book into print, and that she has never received any royalties in the two years it has been on the market.

Full-Service Custom Publisher: A company offering all aspects of publishing, including services such as:

- Transcribing taped sermons
- Ghostwriting
- Substantive editing
- Permissions
- Custom cover design
- Illustrations and special artwork
- Formatting
- ISBN and Library of Congress numbers, copyright submission in author's name
- Printing

Once the book is printed, this type of company offers varying degrees of marketing, promotion, publicity, Internet sales, order fulfillment, warehousing, and distribution. The author funds the production of the book, retains all rights and receives the profit from all the sales. (This would be the best description of WinePress Publishing.)

The upside to full-service custom publishing is:

1. Professional product. Your book can include cover embellishments such as embossing, matte lamination with spot gloss on the title or front cover graphic, and foil or iridescent stamping on the title. With WinePress, professional designers create covers that equal or surpass the standards in the CBA marketplace.

2. An experienced staff helps you through each step of the process. Professional guidance and advice is so important when you take an alternative route to getting your book published. There's a lot of money at stake, and the professionals who walk you through the process help you avoid making costly mistakes.

3. Back-end support allows you to do what you do best. If you have a message you're passionate about, you need to be talking about it, whether it's on the radio, on TV, or at the podium. Only you can sell your message with unique zeal and passion, so why spend your valuable time answering phones, stuffing boxes and running to the post office? We take care of these details so you don't waste your time.

4. Custom publishing is a great way to prove the need for your message to a traditional publisher.

The downside to using a company like WinePress, a full-service book packager, is:

1. It costs more. But remember the old saying, "You get what you pay for."

2. It's still a challenge to get your book on the shelves. We have developed many ways to make up for this issue, such as sending our catalog out directly to 4,500 bookstores; having a booth at the International Christian Retail Show (the Christian Booksellers Association convention held every July), and selling directly to the largest Christian and general market distributors, such as Ingram/Spring Arbor, STL, Anchor, Baker & Taylor, Christianbook.com, and more. We make sure your book is listed with the distributors as well as featuring basic information about your book on "Christian Books & More," a database that bookstores across the country subscribe to as a resource. We even have the connections to help you advertise your book through chain-store catalogs. While this type of program requires a substantial advertising budget, and titles must be approved by a committee, it can virtually guarantee your book on bookstore shelves and create a guaranteed buy of your book on a national basis. Of course, aside from the chain store promotions, no one can guarantee that stores will buy your book and put it on the shelves, but

what we can guarantee is easy accessibility to anyone walking into a bookstore through the special order system each store utilizes. These distributors do not work directly with authors or small publishers with one or two titles only, so it's important to be represented by a publisher like WinePress.

Christian Publicist: A person or company that specializes in booking media interviews for authors on Christian radio and television. Publicists do not sell your book for you; they contact Christian radio and TV talk show hosts and producers and suggest your book as an upcoming topic to be addressed. They schedule as many interviews as possible for authors who have an important message and the ability to communicate it. Some publicists work for a flat fee to promote an entire project, guaranteeing a minimum number of interviews for the fee; others charge a monthly fee plus expenses (shipping copies of your book to producers, long-distance calls, etc.) with a minimum of four to six months to complete the promotional campaign. The WinePress in-house publicity department offers everything from hometown to special market promotions, speaker introductions, build-your-platform campaigns, and more. As a result of the publicity campaigns we offer, WinePress authors have been interviewed by CBN News; Michael Medved; American Family Radio; Janet Parshall's America; Point of View: USA Radio Network; Life Today with James Robeson; The 700 Club, Concerned Women for America; Liberty Counsel; Focus on the Family, and PBS.

The upside to using a publicist:

1. You have an advocate for your book—someone who aggressively pursues exposure for your message.
2. You are able to take advantage of the publicist's relationships, contacts, and media expertise.

The downside to using a publicist:

1. It is an additional expense.

Fulfillment: The activity of receiving inbound telephone inquiries about your book. Typically a toll-free number is supplied, and operators are on duty 24 hours per day. Order processing is completed for people who order using a credit card, and product is packaged and shipped. If customers want to pay by check, the operator gives them the mailing address and total price, including shipping and handling. Product is warehoused by the fulfillment company, which charges a per-piece/per-service item handling charge or deducts a percentage of the selling price from the sales income monthly as a service charge. You will find charges as high as 65 percent and as low as 20 percent.

The WinePress 24-hour order fulfillment service is a great asset for authors who have heavy media exposure or advertising and want to offer the convenience of a toll-free number to their potential customers. Fulfillment is also helpful when a book is not readily available in the bookstore market but needs to be accessible to possible retail customers. The author can promote the book while someone else handles the details of answering phones, taking orders, processing charge cards, packing, shipping, and warehousing. However, remember that the fulfillment company doesn't promote your book—*you* have to make that phone ring!

Christian Booksellers Association (CBA): The professional trade organization to which Christian bookstores and publishers belong. They sponsor the International Christian Retail Show (ICRS), held each July at a different location. At ICRS, publishers exhibit their new product, bookstore buyers come to see the new product, and management and front line workers in the Christian bookstores come for training.

Evangelical Christian Publishers Association (ECPA): A professional trade association specifically for Christian publishers (not bookstores or book buyers). ECPA sponsors the annual Christian Book Awards (formerly known as the Gold Medallion Awards).

American Booksellers Association (ABA): The secular professional trade association that most general market bookstores and publishers belong to. The ABA sponsors the Book Expo, held annually in June.

Christian Book Distributors: Companies that service the Christian bookstore market. Most Christian bookstore buyers are overworked and underpaid, and the last thing they want to do is buy books from every eager author who publishes his own book. For the most part, bookstore owners like to keep things simple: If a book isn't available through one of the major distributors, it isn't worth the hassle of carrying it in the store. Most Christian book distributors are jaded about carrying self-published books, and rightly so. Many self-published books look self-published; and if a book looks bad, it can't compete on the shelves of a Christian bookstore next to a book by someone like Max Lucado, whose publisher spends $3,000 or more to create a cover that jumps off the shelf and into the customer's hand.

The bottom line is that it is not easy to have your book picked up by a distributor. While we at WinePress have contracts with all the major Christian book distributors, we suggest that the distributors order larger quantities only of titles that have the ability to compete nationally. The author must have a timely topic, the ability to communicate effectively via the media, and have a decent advertising/publicity budget.

Most distributors expect a 55 to 60 percent discount. If a self-published author prints fewer than 3,500 copies, he cannot afford to give the discount required without going in the red on distributor sales. All the more reason to have other sales channels where you don't have to give away such a large discount. Speaking engagements and direct selling online from your Web site through grassroots marketing are the best examples of alternate sales channels.

CHAPTER 6

Budgeting Your Project

. . . .

BEFORE YOU START working on a budget for your project you need to thought-fully ask yourself, "How many books should I print?" Typically, first-time authors overestimate rather than underestimate their sales. I would rather see someone print 1,500 or 2,500 copies and have to print more, than print 5,000 or 10,000 and end up with a garage full of books. However, if the market is there for your book, it's also important to know that printing 2,500 copies and then reprinting another 2,500 copies is much more expensive than starting with 5,000 to begin with. So how many should you start with? Ask yourself the following questions:

1. Do you have an audience?
2. How are you going to reach them?
3. Are there any publications that zero in on that particular group?
4. Is your topic cutting edge or old news?
5. Are there any ministries or nonprofit organizations that promote a message similar to the one in your book?
6. Are you considered an expert in your field? (You don't have to have a Ph.D.)
7. Do you currently do any public speaking?
8. Have you done radio or TV interviews in the past?
9. Do you communicate effectively?

10. Do you have access to a mailing list of people who would need your book? (Targeted mailing lists are available for purchase, but you may already have a mailing list from your ministry activities, speaking engagements, etc.)

11. Do you have any other distribution channels through which your book might be sold?

12. Are you willing to spend additional money to promote and market your book?

By asking yourself these questions, you can get a feel for the number of books you should print. If the majority of your answers were *no*, you may want to consider going the print-on-demand route. If nothing else, you will get your message out to a limited degree and will have fulfilled—without a huge financial outlay—the calling God had for you to get it into print.

If you answered *yes* to at least three of these questions, you should seriously consider printing 2,500 copies. If you gave a positive answer to six or more of the questions, I would suggest printing from 5,000 to 10,000 copies, which would give you the best rate per copy. Remember, the higher the quantity, the lower the price per copy.

The print-on-demand option gives authors an affordable way to test the market before committing to buying a large inventory of books. However, since we've recently reduced the minimum print run for a WinePress run, it often makes more sense to start with an offset run if at all possible. Why?

The upside to beginning with an offset print run with WinePress is as follows:

1. No limitations on binding, trim size, or any out of the box-type specifications.

2. Specialty bindings such as lay flat, board books, wire-O, leather, CD or DVD inserts, a reply card inserted into the back, or gift boxes.

3. Cover embellishments like matte & spot gloss lamination, embossing or foil stamping, or French flaps. Since people do judge a book by its cover, having these kinds of extra bells and whistles added to a beautifully designed cover really *can* made a difference.

4. Unique paper types available such as Bible paper with gold gilded edges, or cream stock with frayed edges can make your book a true "one of a kind" product.

5. The design for the interior of your book is completely customized to the approved front cover. This enables our designers the opportunity to get creative with the formatting of your book, using images and fonts from the front cover throughout the entirety of the book.

6. You have the prestige of the WinePress imprint. Since the WinePress name has been around since 1991, it's much better known than our print-on-demand imprint.

7. The credibility of having a large print run communicates commitment on your part. This can speak volumes to those you come in contact with.

8. The solid feel of an offset printed book (there really is a difference!)

9. Special promotional options, such as national chain store representation (more on this mentioned in Chapter 9).

10. When you begin with a large print run, you are able to set your Suggested Retail Price.

11. The more you print, the lower the cost per copy. A large print run means you can give large discounts to distributors, which results in higher profit margins and a better return.

12. Product is always on hand in our warehouse, and through all the possible Christian distributors in the marketplace.

The downside to beginning with a large print run is:

1. Obviously, there's a larger initial cost.
2. And as with any outlay, there's a bigger risk involved.

The upside to starting with our print-on-demand option with Pleasant Word is:

1. A lower initial expense.
2. No warehousing, as books are printed as needed, literally one at a time.
3. Since the initial cost is smaller, the risk is lower.
4. Of course, if you know your market is only going to be a few hundred readers, then this would be the only way to go!

The downside to starting with print-on-demand:

1. Your options are limited regarding trim size, paper choices, and bindings.
2. The only option for your cover is high gloss lamination.
3. Your text is formatted utilizing your choice of pre-designed format options.

4. Your price per book, should you sell 1500 or more copies, would be more than you'd pay for a larger print run.

5. In some circles, POD lacks credibility. Unfortunately, this is due to other unprofessional POD publishers who produce low-quality product and do not offer standard trade discounts.

6. Some bookstore chains actually refuse to schedule booksignings if they know your book is POD. This, I'm sure, is due to some of those same POD companies being slow in filling orders so that stores cannot be sure they will have inventory for their event dates. Hence, blanket policies are put in place due to other companies leaving buyers with a bad taste in their mouths.

7. The Suggested Retail Price is higher than normal due to the economics of printing books one at a time.

All that said, if your only option is to start with print-on-demand, then it is certainly a great way to get started and prove that there's a market for your work. It's definitely worth pondering the pros and cons of each option before you make your final determination. As always, our solutions advisors specialize in helping authors make the right decision.

When working up your budget to publish your book, you'll need to think about a number of things:

1. Cost per book, (must include adequate editing, proofreading, formatting, cover design, ISBN, copyrights, and printing).

2. Reprint cost per book (assuming no changes to cover or interior, or also with a cost per page of corrections. It's good to know reprint costs so you can make long-term projections about how profitable your project will be.

3. Cost for overruns (all commercial printing has a ten percent margin that is legally billable to the client. This means you could end up with ten percent more books than you originally ordered, and you are required to pay for those additional books, but at a lower rate per copy. If the printer prints more than ten percent over your order, the additional copies are yours at no charge. This is a standard in the industry and is unavoidable. Over the last two years, our average overrun has been about five percent, but on occasion a full ten percent is received. It's best to be prepared to cover the entire ten percent rather than expecting five percent and ending up with the full ten!

4. Cost to have the book shipped to you or to your publisher's warehouse.

5. Mailing costs for promotional materials (postage, purchase of a mailing list, printing of fliers or postcards).

6. Advertising costs (specifically targeted magazine or newsletter advertising, cooperative advertising, advertising to bookstores through distributors).

7. Phone bills for long distance calls for radio interviews.

8. Publicity services can range anywhere from a few thousand on the low end to a $25,000 flat fee for some secular publicists. If you're trying to gain national exposure, I recommend earmarking somewhere between $5,000 and $45,000 on publicity if funds allow and it makes good sense. Keep in mind that most royalty publishers spend from $25,000 to $75,000 (sometimes as much as $500,000 to $1 million!) on publicity and marketing to launch a new book.

9. Discount given to bookstores (30–45 percent off the retail price).

10. Discount given to distributors (55–60 percent off the retail price).

12. Warehousing and fulfillment fees.

13. The retail price of your book must be high enough so you can give the needed discounts, but not so high that you lose buyers because of it.

Depending on the quantity of your print run, the type of binding, the page count, and the amount of editing required, you could pay anywhere from $1.25 to $20 per copy.

Now let's think through what you can afford to do in the discount department. If you want to make your book available to bookstores through distributors, you'll need to be willing to give away 55 percent of the cover price. If you charge $10 for your 96-page book, you will net $4.50 before any fulfillment fees are assessed. What that means is you probably won't break even on 2,500 copies, and could end up losing money giving that large a discount. But on 5,000 to 10,000 copies, you stand to make a profit on sales to distributors. Of course, you will make much more on sales directly to bookstores (they only get a 30–40 percent discount), through your Web site, or via sales made at the back of the room when you are speaking in churches or at local or national events.

But keep in mind, online bookstores such as Amazon.com, BarnesandNoble.com, Borders.com, Booksamillion.com and others have all made a shift to purchasing *only* product that is available through Ingram or Baker & Taylor, so if you want your book to be available online in the well-known stores, you have to be willing to give away that 55 percent off the retail price.

Recently, someone asked if I would work up some numbers to show the difference in potential earnings when publishing with WinePress versus a royalty publisher. As I worked the numbers, I was amazed at how much more an author stands to earn by going the non-traditional route—with a company like WinePress that offers all the services of a royalty publisher. Here's the bottom line: If you were to start off with a 10,000-book print run and sell approximately 4,000 copies direct at your speaking engagements, 2,000 copies through our fulfillment service, 2,000 directly to bookstores or ministries through our warehouse, and 2,000 to distributors or wholesalers, your net profit would be somewhere around $80,000. The same quantity sold through a royalty publisher would net you $40,000—a $40,000 difference!

If you were to choose our print-on-demand option you could spend anywhere from $1,000 to $10,000, depending on your word count, the level of editing required, and the level of marketing and publicity services you start with (the average being somewhere around $3,000-$5,000). You could break even by selling anywhere from 200 copies to 700 copies, and then, if it makes sense, upgrade to a large print run where the numbers become even more profitable.

CHAPTER 7

Raising Funds for Your Book Project

. . . .

ONE THING I know for sure, our God owns the cattle on a thousand hills, and He's not broke! If He has called you to self-publish, He surely will provide the funds for you to do so. And if He doesn't provide a large sum to start off with 1,500 or more books, print-on-demand is always a great way to begin.

I've seen Him do some miraculous financing to ensure that His children get His message into print. Maggie Kubo contemplated taking out a loan to publish her children's book, *The Land of Broken Rainbows.* Right before she went that route, she received an unexpected inheritance that covered the exact cost of publishing her book!

Jay Zinn put together a group of investors who believed in his end-times novel, *The Unveiling.* He promised them each a portion of the profits once the principal was paid back. He's completely sold out the first printing of 8,000.

Audrey Nally didn't know how she would come up with the money to publish her children's book, *In Heaven.* Out of the blue, her grandmother gave her a check for $10,000 to help her get the book published.

Claire Vomhof had planned to publish his book of poetry for years but didn't have the funding. A terminally ill man he knew offered to pay for the publishing so Claire's dream could become a reality. The man died before he was able to give Claire the money, but his brother stepped up to the plate and donated the amount needed to get it into print.

Michele Rickett applied for a small business loan to publish her mentoring curriculum, *Ordinary Women.* She lined up enough speaking engagements to prove to the bank that the amount she was borrowing would easily be paid back within the first six months her workbook was available for sale.

Just recently, one very excited writer called me after waiting four years for the funding for her book. Someone had given her a raffle ticket to a $15,000 kitchen makeover. Just a few moments later, she was announced as the winner. However, there were not enough tickets sold to provide the makeover. Instead the organization gave her all the money from the raffle. The total amount was within $5 of what she needed to get her project going with Pleasant Word. I could go on and on, but suffice it to say, He is able.

A number of our authors, who have not had the few thousand dollars it takes to get a quality print-on-demand project published, have treated their book project like a mission trip. They've written letters to family, friends, and business associates asking for "sponsors" for their project. Their published book contains a page that thanks those whose generous contributions made the book possible.

One WinePress author successfully raised a large portion of the money needed by sending out a letter to over 900 ministry contacts he'd developed over his many years as a pastor. In his letter, Paul Tribus offered to donate a copy of his book, *How to Overcome Bitterness, Anger and Unforgiveness* to an incarcerated veteran for every donation of $15 he received. From that one letter he raised over $7500. While those on his mailing list may not have purchased the book for themselves, the idea of providing a free copy to someone in prison was very appealing.

If you start off with print-on-demand and find that your book has a large enough market to warrant a large print run, you may need to come up with some creative financing. A number of years ago I heard an interview with promoter and television producer Harry Green on this very topic. I pray that the ideas he shares are helpful to you.

Aside from any personal resources you may have, there are essentially three ways to generate capital to fund your project. They are sales, debt, and equity.

If you are fortunate enough to be able to get advance orders for your product, you could fund your project with revenues produced by the sales. Because this is usually not possible, debt and equity funding represent the most-used capital raising alternatives.

Debt—Borrowing Money

Many people borrow money to finance their projects. Some people use their credit cards; others the equity line on their home; and some people borrow the money from friends, relatives, or a bank or credit union. If your motive for sharing your gift or producing your product is strictly to make money or to pay bills, you are headed for trouble. Everyone I have worked with who has elected to go this route has just dug themselves in deeper. Producing and marketing your product takes time, patience, and perseverance. Borrowing money can impose timetables on your project that are unrealistic or are unattainable. Moreover, if you borrow from friends or relatives you can really strain your relationships if things do not go as expected. If your family or friends want to help you, you're better off having them as investors and using an equity form of financing. This form of funding will define your relationship in a formal document and will clearly point out the financial risks and rewards inherent in their involvement in your project.

Equity Funding

If structured properly, an equity arrangement with investors who share your vision can be the best method of funding your project. Under this arrangement, you essentially sell a percentage of future revenue or ownership of your project in exchange for the money for production and marketing. This arrangement could be structured in the form of a limited partnership or a closely held corporation. Provisions for establishing partnerships and corporations vary by state. You should work with an attorney to establish the appropriate vehicle for your situation.

I believe that the limited partnership offers the most attractive source of funding for the entrepreneur who is an author, musical artist, or creative product producer. It provides unlimited flexibility for structuring percentage payback to investors while enabling the product creator or talent to maintain control or ownership. It also provides a formalized structure that appeals to investors.

The typical arrangement that appeals to investors involves paying them back their initial investment out of the first sales that are generated. Once they have regained their principal investment, their percentage is reduced to 10 or 15 percent of sales or profits while you retain the balance. This type of arrangement reduces the investors risk and enables them to participate in the long-term success of the project. Astute investors are always looking to reduce their downside risk and increase their upside potential. When you structure your deal, don't be greedy!

Try to get investors who can help you with more than money. People who believe in you who are constantly selling you are a great asset. People who put their "money where their mouth is" are by far the ultimate asset.

The limited partnership can also offer tax advantages to some investors. Your investors should seek the counsel of a good CPA or tax planner before you finalize the structure of your partnership. In this area, good advice is important. Don't try to save money by doing it yourself without the counsel of qualified professionals.

In addition to limited partnerships, there are a variety of corporate structures that can be considered as funding vehicles. I prefer partnerships in that they offer attractive methods for distributing revenues without selling the company or declaring dividends that could involve double taxation. The motion picture industry has been using partnerships for years to finance movies.

I cannot over-emphasize the importance of seeking qualified counsel in structuring a financial relationship. Most states enable you to raise up to $1 million without registering your fund-raising instrument with the Securities and Exchange Commission.

Situations that involve fewer than fifteen investors are also usually exempt from such registrations.

Creating the right fund-raising vehicle is not as complicated as it may seem and is one of the most important steps you can take in ensuring the success of your project. Some attorneys and accountants may work with you on a percentage basis and provide services you need for a "piece of the action." Do not be afraid to ask . . . but don't expect it. I have learned the hard way that you get what you pay for.

Once you have established your financial arrangement and secured capital from your investors, it is important that you continue to communicate with your investors on a regular basis. Keep them apprised of your progress. Call them regularly or send them a newsletter. Share the good news and the bad news. Don't make them call you. More importantly, when you achieve success... if you achieve success... don't forget who brought you to the dance.

While I used to include a basic document showing the legal wording used in creating a partnership like this, I've deleted it from this edition because there really is no cookie-cutter way to do it. The best advice I can give you is to take your ideas for the LLC and work with an attorney you trust to draw up the paperwork. That way, what you have will be based on the laws of your state and the current SEC regulations regarding limited liability corporations.

Now we'll take a look at some things you can do during the publishing process.

CHAPTER 8

Pre-Publication Promotion

. . . .

I T IS IMPORTANT to think about promotion during the production phase rather than waiting until cartons of books are unloaded at your doorstep or at our warehouse.

Get the Word Out

While you are writing your book you should be getting the word out. Tell everyone you know what you are writing about. Get people praying for you and your project. If you know people at your local Christian bookstore, let them know what you are working on and when you plan to have your book completed. Start mentioning the book on your blog or Web site and get the buzz going.

Input

You want your message to be clear and your book to be the best possible, so during the writing and editing process, seek opinions, constructive criticism, testimonials, reviews, and comments. Don't be close-minded or adamant that your message is exactly how God wants it written. Numerous rewrites are often necessary to ensure that your message is crystal clear. Go to people you trust (don't throw your pearls before swine!) and ask for their input. But remember, they also know you, so they have the benefit of knowing your story and filling in where you are silent. That's why I highly recommend having a professional critique done as part of your editing. A professional, *who does not know you*, can point out holes and weak areas. A professional critique comes with all WinePress packages that include substantive edits or coaching.

Once the manuscript seems close to completion, start collecting written reviews and testimonials from the people who read it. Be sure you receive written permission from them if you plan to use their comments in your sales material.

Be willing to spend extra money on a substantive edit. During a substantive edit, a professional editor looks closely at your content, points out holes that need to be filled, and moves things around so your manuscript communicates as effectively as possible. A great cover and beautiful formatting job won't cover up poor writing.

We understand some people want an editor to use their professional skills to improve the manuscript. This constitutes more of a re-write. While more expensive, it is perfect for those who are too busy to spend more time on the manuscript. Other authors want to learn during the editing process and have a more hands-on approach. An extensive amount of back-and-forth mentoring is available in our Special Coaching package, so you can improve your skills as you improve the manuscript.

Here are 21 tips to better writing (from the editors at WinePress):

1. Determine the purpose of your writing and explain it in one sentence. Make that purpose the "red thread" that funnels throughout your manuscript.

2. Determine your audience. Write to that person as if he or she is sitting in front of you.

3. Plan your writing and focus on organization.

4. Write an opening or lead that immediately "hooks" the reader. Use an anecdote, a fact, some dialogue, or a quote to grab the reader's attention. A great hook is critical for the first chapter, but is also important for every chapter in your book.

5. Write in simple sentences. Vary the length of your sentences and paragraphs. Watch out for *sentence fragments* (a group of words without a complete thought), *run-on sentences* (two sentences joined together without punctuation or a connecting word), and *rambling sentences* (too many short phrases connected with *and*).

6. To emphasize a word or phrase, put it at the beginning or end of a sentence or paragraph.

7. Choose a viewpoint and write consistently in that viewpoint.

8. Show; don't tell. Use dialogue, descriptive words, and all the senses to show what happens.

9. Use the *active voice* rather than the *passive voice*. The *dog bit* the man, instead of: The *man was bit* by the dog.

10. Use concrete nouns and action verbs. Instead of saying "East Coast city," say *New York*. Look for "be" verbs—is, am, was, were, be, should, etc.—and replace with stronger verbs. (Instead of writing, *He was tired,* write, *His taut muscles screamed for a reprieve from shoveling dirt.*)

11. Use dialogue to draw the reader into your writing. Each new speaker gets a new paragraph. Use italics—not quotation marks—for thoughts. Don't attribute every line of dialogue with a "said so and so." Use an attribution only when you need to clarify who is speaking.

12. Avoid slang, jargon, and clichés.

13. Stay to the point. Don't veer off on rabbit trails. Write tight!

14. Pick a short, catchy title that explains the book's purpose. Sometimes a subtitle helps to explain the title.

15. Choose a verb tense and stick with it.

16. Check, double-check, and triple-check spelling, punctuation, and grammar. Don't rely on your computer's spell checker to do the job for you; spell checkers often don't recognize homophones (there/they're/their, piece/peace). Grammar and usage rules change frequently, so invest in a good style book and consult it regularly.

17. Ask someone besides your best friend, spouse, or mother to read your writing and give honest suggestions for improvement.

18. Verify the accuracy of all facts and quotations. Especially take care to quote the Bible correctly (noting which translation(s) you use). Cite all sources using correct endnote format.

19. Use the proper format when submitting a manuscript.

20. Use strong transitions between paragraphs so your thoughts flow logically from one idea to the next.

21. Stop when you reach the end. When you know that your purpose has been accomplished, it's time to stop and e-mail your manuscript.

If you are still in the idea stage or organizing stage of writing your manuscript, this additional information may be some encouragement for you as you put your manuscript together.

Once you've determined the purpose of your book, the one key thing you want the reader to walk away with—we call that the "red thread"—put an outline together. Each point in your outline will become a chapter.

Then consider the following integral elements of a well-rounded manuscript: *communication, education, illustration, and citation.*

Communication:

Have you ever read a book or listened to a speaker and asked yourself, "And her point is…?" Clearly communicate your main point and sub-points. And don't worry; if you're too direct or blunt, the editor can help soften it up.

Education:

Educate your reader how to apply the information you are sharing. This ensures you are giving your reader "take away" value. Consider adding discussion questions to the end of each chapter, so your book becomes a resource for small groups.

Illustration:

Use your personal experience or tell someone else's story to illustrate your point. Stories bring the manuscript to life and help the reader relate. It's no longer just theory or your opinion; it's proof that what you are saying is backed up with action. You've lived it, and you can relate to your reader. This is also where you use dialogue and description to draw the reader in.

Citation:

Show the validity of your message using scriptures, articles from a magazine or newspaper, statistics, one of the classics, or quotes from a book or a well known person. It's not enough to just use *your* experience; you need to back it up with scripture or a quote . . . someone else saying the same thing in different words. This brings credibility to your manuscript.

When your outline is finished, start writing. Don't edit yourself, don't critique yourself. *Just write.* Leave all the detail, polishing and fine tuning to our editors.

For every double-spaced page (12-point font, 1-inch margins all around), you should end up with one page in a finished book. So, if you want a 150-page book, shoot for 150 double-spaced pages, or approximately 37,500 words.

Suggested writing tools

The Write Start: Practical Advice for Successful Writing (Pleasant Word, a division of WinePress Publishing). Available through www.upwritebooks.com.

Polishing the PUGS: Punctuation, Usage, Grammar and Spelling Tips for Writers, by Kathy Ide (Upwrite Books, a division of WinePress Publishing). Available through www.upwritebooks.com.

Chicago Manual of Style (The University of Chicago Press). Available in the library or from any bookstore. We recommend using the latest version of this regularly-updated style manual.

Children's Writer's Word Book by Alijandra Mogliner (Writer's Digest Books). A must-have if you write for children.

Writing Dramatic Non-Fiction, by William Noble (Writer's Digest Books).

Book Production

Now it is time to begin the production process. Submit your manuscript to a reputable book packager or to a consultant, such as WinePress, for a quote. After researching your options, start the process with the company that offers you a fair price for a high-quality product and the services you need.

I would go one step further; I would get into the prayer closet and ask the Lord who He wants you to work with. It may not be the company with the lowest price or the best sales pitch. It's important, no matter what you do, to hear God's voice about whom to work with.

First, you will need a cover design so you have a visual to use for your sales literature. As I mentioned earlier, the WinePress cover designers produce top-notch covers that look like the "big guys" and give your message the creditability it deserves. As your book is going through the editing, formatting, and printing process, you will want to talk it up to everyone you know.

While we're on the subject of covers, let's think through not only the front cover but the back cover, as well. Here are some great tips adapted from a workshop titled, "Cover Design, Titling, and Writing Sales Copy," by Ken Petersen (formerly with Tyndale House Publishers, ECPA Annual Conference 2001):

Book Cover Ideas

One of the biggest challenges for publishers is getting the attention of the buyer. Since buyers see the cover first, it is imperative to make it stand out. Please consider the following points as you think about your cover design. Keep in mind that these suggestions came from professionals with years of experience in the book publishing industry. Their advice will keep your book competitive with those from traditional publishing houses.

Distinctiveness: Find one unique feature about your book.
The more distinct your cover, the more likely someone will pick it up and turn to the back cover copy. Here are some tips:

1. Simplify. The entire book cannot be represented on the cover.
2. Write a paragraph about one unique aspect of your book. Have one or two other people do the same, without your input. This will give you a more objective analysis.
3. Condense these paragraphs into one sentence.
4. Look for a catchy phrase that captures the uniqueness of the book.
5. Sometimes the author or the organization is the unique thing.

Categorization: Where does your book fit?
Cover illustrations categorize a book. Readers know what to look for by the illustrations. To understand book covers and categorization, go to a bookstore and study the books in each section. You will find the following similar characteristics in the books:

- Historical fiction books have landscapes that run over the spine of the book, creating a sweeping effect like the passing of time. The illustrations include people and scenery that are era appropriate.
- Thrillers have big type, icon images, and dark backgrounds.
- Self-help books often have a picture of the author, light background, and big type.
- Business books generally have no imagery, primary colors, and very large type.
- Christian Living gives a spiritual promise in the title or sales copy, such as "When God Whispers Your Name," or "The Power of a Praying Wife."

- Look at the books in the same category as your own book.

Techniques: Quiz yourself with questions about your book. This will help you discover things that the BUYER looks for. Keep the reader in mind—the cover needs to catch the customer's attention, not just contain a picture *you* like. Answer the following questions from the reader's viewpoint:

- Why do I need this book?
- What is at the heart of the buyer?
- What's broken and needs to be fixed?
- Why is this the best book on the subject?
- What's the main message the cover portrays to the average person, without reading the text?

Also, try the following techniques:

1. Come up with key words. Write as many as you can think of randomly on paper and pull them together in combinations to find a title or subtitle that works.
2. If your manuscript has headers, look for a title in your list of words.
3. Sometimes scripture provides title or sales copy.

Back Cover Copy: Again, visit a bookstore and read lots of back covers in your book's category. Back cover copy is never written in first person or passively. It is always active, as if it's speaking to the person reading it. People want to know how your book will help them. For example, do not say, "I wrote this book because I want you to know my experiences with God." Instead something like this grips the reader: "Discover how to deepen your relationship with God through the experiences chronicled in *Built on the Rock*." Think of catchy bulleted points. A fiction back cover needs to give enough of the plot to intrigue the reader but still leave them "dangling" so they have a reason to buy the book.

A buyer never reads the entire back cover, but anywhere their eyes land on the page must tell them about your book. For this reason it's a good idea to have a one sentence description, short endorsements and bullets, along with the main description of the book. Your bio should also be very pointed, not your life story from birth.

Worksheet for Writing Back Cover

Ask these questions:

- Is my book life-changing?
- Ageless? Timeless?
- What response does it evoke?

Fill in the blanks:

My book _____ is about _____

_____

Now think about a buyer who would be looking for your topic:

This buyer is a _____ walking into a _____
_____and he/she will pick up, buy or read my book
because _____

My book is similar to _____ but better or different
because _____

Now write the back cover from these three sentences. Use them for marketing your book.

Back cover copy should have THREE PARTS or THREE PARAGRAPHS.

1. A Great Sales Pitch
   a. Identify your audience.
   b. Explain why the reader cannot live without this book.
   c. Convey the heartfelt need or the "want to" or "need to" of this idea.
   d. Pitch the take-away of the book.

2. Mechanics of the Book
   a. Nuts & bolts paragraph, which can be bulleted. Bullets help the reader quickly and concisely know what your book is about.

      b. How will this book feel, taste, smell, look?

      c. Will it have steps, anecdotes, how tos?

3. The Author Bio Paragraph

      a. Who is the author and why should the reader care?

      b. Don't include your dog's name (unless the book is about the dog), or your hobbies (unless the book is about the hobby).

      c. List expertise, writing credits, community and ministry connections related to the book's topic.

      d. This paragraph will draw the reader to you, the author. Convince the reader that you are the expert or have a great story to tell.

      e. Leave small details about where you live, with whom (spouse and 10 kids), non-related occupation information, etc., for the 1–2 sentence bio next to your picture.

Use words like:

- Practical
- Proven
- Numbers
- Simple
- Must-have

Remember:

- Use your strong points!
- Keep your audience in mind!
- This is your first contact with the reader!
- Keep it simple!
- Watch for redundancies!
- Write tight!

Price

It's a good idea to set a competitive retail price. Research similar products offered in local Christian bookstores. One complaint bookstores have regarding self-published books is that they are typically overpriced. This is understandable when you realize how much some people have had to pay to get the job done (and often times not well enough to even sell out the first printing!) At WinePress, we suggest that people use the following guideline:

48 to 64 pages:	$8.99
65 to 96 pages:	$9.99
97 to 128 pages:	$11.99
129 to 160 pages:	$12.99
161 to 192 pages:	$13.99
193 to 240 pages:	$14.99
241 to 288 pages:	$16.99
289 to 356 pages:	$17.99–$18.99
357 to 408 pages:	$19.99–$21.99

Of course, if you choose to go the print-on-demand route, you give up the right to set your retail price; that becomes the publisher's right. Retail prices for our print-on-demand books are usually only about $2 more than our suggested WinePress prices.

A secular print-on-demand company sets their prices based on page counts as follows:

Under 100 pages:	$15.99
101 to 399 pages:	$19.99
400 to 799 pages:	$23.99

These prices are quite a bit higher than the suggested retail prices I've listed, which are right in line with the prices you'll normally pay at a Christian bookstore.

We've made a point with our POD division to keep retail prices as reasonable as possible. The last thing you want to do is have your book priced so high that no one will buy it! On our bookstore site we automatically offer our print-on-demand titles at a 27 percent discount so the price is competitive with Amazon's. Book buyers pay the same low price at our site as they would on Amazon, and the author earns a royalty that is three times more than if someone bought the book from Amazon.

Authors of some of our ministry titles set their price at "any donation of $9 or more." It is amazing how many people will give $10, $20, $50, and even $100 for one book. If you are in the ministry full time, this is a great way to set the price of your book.

If you're going to be doing a lot of back-of-the-room sales after speaking engagements, you might set your price to one round figure that includes any applicable sales tax—such as, $10 or $20. This facilitates making change. In the seminar arena you can usually charge more for your book, and it will still sell because it is not competing with a hundred other books in a bookstore.

If you plan to sell your book mainly through a toll-free number or by mail order, you'll want to consider keeping the price lower. That way, the total price—including your shipping and handling charge—won't scare off your customer.

Pre-publication Order Form

With your cover design complete, write some promotional material for a sales flier. Include pre-publication ordering information, which offers buyers an incentive to purchase a copy before your book is published. Some authors offer a 15-to-25 percent discount and free shipping if people pay in advance to order the book.

At WinePress, we can create a pre-publication or sales flier that includes the intended page count of the book, its retail price, ISBN, cover artwork, and an overview with reviews and comments. We also include the pre-publication discount information and cutoff date, along with other ordering information. This is a great resource for authors to use to raise money while in the production process.

Pastor Ray Hampton started his project for a large print run at WinePress with a 50 percent down payment on book production costs. Then, using a pre-publication order form, he raised the balance through pre-publication sales. He was pleasantly surprised to discover how quickly he was able to cover the remaining cost of his project.

Press Releases to Local Media

Media exposure is a great way to get free advertising for your book. When creating your press release, focus on how your book will benefit the reader. Work hard at encapsulating the content into 100 words or less, emphasizing the importance of your book's thesis.

I always encourage authors to memorize a 40-word-or-less explanation of their book, highlighting the benefits to the reader. Everyone wants to know, "What's in it for me?"

While the book's content is important, the most essential questions readers have are:

- What will this book do for me?
- What problem will it solve?
- What questions will it answer?
- What benefits will it offer?

A one-page press release needs to contain a newsworthy angle so it grabs the attention of the targeted producer or reporter. But a compelling angle does no good all alone. Without prompt and persistent follow up, it's all wasted effort. That's why our in-house publicity department works hard at following up with the media to make sure you get the exposure you need.

When an author works with our in-house publicists, we custom-design a campaign that fits the author's personality and book. We offer many different campaigns that can be mixed and matched to most benefit the author and his or her message. Our publicity campaigns work well for fiction, non-fiction, introverts, extroverts—even niche and special markets.

Page Proofs to Reviewers

If you are printing 5,000 or more copies, have committed to a publicity campaign, and have an advertising budget/plan to make your book available in the Christian bookstore market, then it is a good idea to have a copy of your page proofs (the typeset version of your manuscript) and a sample cover sent to appropriate book reviewers. "Appropriate" means that if you are writing a book on moms leaving the workplace to stay home and raise their children, we wouldn't send your proofs to the book review editor for *Discipleship Journal*; we would send them to *Today's Christian Woman*.

It's not easy to obtain a review, so don't get your hopes up that this is where all your sales are going to come from. I am cautious in encouraging first-time authors toward this end, because the market is very competitive. At the 2007 Mt. Hermon Christian Writers Conference, Rebeca Seitz of Glass Road Public Relations made the point that reviewers and bloggers do not review self-published books. Rebeca's company represents some of the biggest names in Christian fiction for some of the most well known royalty publishers. She went on to say that WinePress is the *only* self-publisher she represents to reviewers because we are known for producing credible, quality product.

Some book reviewers are picky about how they receive page proofs. They want them long before the book is released. Some even want them trimmed and bound. Again, unless you are printing 5,000 to 10,000 copies and will be doing some major promotion through the larger Christian book distributors and industry publications, I wouldn't spend a lot of time trying to get reviews in national Christian publications. You may, however, want to approach your local Christian newspaper to see if they would be interested in conducting an interview with you, using an excerpt from the book, or writing their own book review. Also, the religion editor for your local daily or weekly newspaper often does book reviews.

Distribution Schedule

This step can be a Catch-22. If you are self-published, most Christian book distributors will not look at your book. Spring Arbor Distributors tells self-published authors that it will take six months before they will even look at the finished product, and even then, you should not count on them to pick it up. Unfortunately, authors who have created shoddy, unprofessional products have made it hard on the rest of us. Because WinePress is committed to the publicity and promotion of appropriate (truly marketable) titles, and because of our reputation of producing high-quality products, we have gained access to the major distributors. We have set up contracts with them to distribute all our titles, as long as the author is willing to extend a 55 percent discount.

We also work with other distributors who choose the titles they will offer. Landing a Christian book distributor on your own is not altogether impossible, but very close to it. That's one very good reason to publish your book with WinePress! We've gone to the expense and trouble to contract with the major distributors at a 55 percent discount and the distributor pays the freight charges, rather than the author. This makes it much more affordable for our authors to make their books available to bookstores.

Direct Mail Campaign

If you believe that the Lord wants you to promote and market your book by purchasing a mailing list of prospective buyers, don't wait too long to get started. My favorite direct mail campaign is using postcards. Once your cover artwork is completed, it can be used on the four-color glossy side of the postcard. The other side should have a short description of the book and a reason why people should buy it, along with simple ordering information: a toll-free number or an address, retail price, and shipping and handling charges.

The preference for using postcards is backed up by statistics. A *Better Homes and Gardens* survey found that an average of 17 people read every postcard sent through the mail. That means 16 people read your postcard before it actually gets to where it's going. That's great exposure!

Fulfillment Services

You probably have a day job and a life other than authoring. If you want to promote your book and not worry about the details of taking and filling orders, then you need a fulfillment service, which we offer as a benefit to our authors. While some companies charge 50-to-65 percent, WinePress rates range from 20-to-35 percent of the amount we receive in payment for your book—among the lowest in the industry.

If you're shopping around for a company to publish and provide fulfillment services, do your homework and learn what services the fees include, and what costs extra. One self-publishing company touts a sales force that will sell your books to bookstores (unfortunately, we have found that these companies over-promise and under-deliver). The catch is that you have to give away 65 percent in fulfillment fees, even when consumers order your book directly from the publisher.

Book Signings

Once a release date for your book is set, start organizing book signings with local Christian bookstores, your church, or other affiliated organizations. Sometimes Christian bookstores will have a Local Authors' Day, where they invite several local authors in for a two- to four-hour period to autograph copies of their books. The store promotes the event in the community so people can come in to meet the authors and buy autographed books. If your local Christian bookstore hasn't done this, suggest it to them. Another great idea is a signing event with a theme. These can create great energy and draw large crowds. Our local bookstore was one of the stops for the Motiv8 Fantasy Fiction Tour. Eight well known Christian fantasy fiction authors spent a week stopping at two bookstores a day up and down the West Coast. There were medieval costumes, sword fights, lots of fun and tons of books sold! To see a video of the event visit www.fantasyfictiontour.com and search back to Day 1 Seattle.

Some of our authors have set up publication parties, where they send out invitations to everyone they know. They make it a festive event. You may have friends who want to have a signing party in their home so they can invite all their friends over to meet you and hear about your book. Through scheduling events, you'll find many opportunities to share the message the Lord has given you.

Here's a great article on creating a powerful book launch:

There is no doubt that the day when you finally hold your book in your hands is one of the happiest days for a writer. After so many months—if not years—of writing, revising, editing, submitting, and finally, publishing, you can see and touch your baby. This occasion calls for a big celebration and what better way to send this book off unto the hands of your readers than with a Book Launch Party.

One of the main considerations for this party is that you probably thought of it way back when you were planning to write the book. The book marketing plan must be prepared before the book itself in order to ensure success. Considering the topic and audience of the book determines the theme of the party along with all the activities. The best days to do a Book Launch Party are either Friday or Saturday, in order to get the most attendance. The time of day has a lot to do with the theme; it could easily be a picnic at the beach as a wine and cheese or masquerade during the evening.

Here are the key ingredients on The Ultimate Book Launch Party:

Theme: Select a theme directly related to your book. Fiction books are excellent in this regard.

Invitations: Create one-of-a-kind invitations for the launch. You can get an inexpensive software program and design and print your own invitations. Request to RSVP.

News & Media: Prepare a news release to mark the event and forward it to your local newspaper at least four to six weeks in advance. Do not forget to send a personal invitation to your local news person.

Party Register: Have everyone register on your party register and include their e-mail and mailing address. Tell them they will be the first to know about your next book sale, book release, contests, and giveaways.

Game or Contest: Create a game or contest around your book.

Food & Drinks: Have something simple to offer your guests on elegant serving plates.

Reading: Read portions of your book or better yet, have some of your guests read a short portion of it. If anyone assisting has read your book, ask them to tell the others about it. Nothing sells more than a satisfied reader.

Pictures: Take plenty of pictures with your guests while the party is going on. You might want to give the camera to one of them to take pictures as you visit with everyone there. The pictures will be great for promotional materials, Web sites and blogs*.

*Note: You might want to have a release form ready for all the attendants to sign to authorize posting their pictures online or in printed materials without compensation.

Sell: Offer special discounts to your guests who buy two or more signed copies of your book. Have bookmarks, flyers and mail order forms for everyone so those who do not buy can order later. For those who do not buy on the spot, offer the same special discount if they order in the next 48 hours.

Follow Up: Send the guests a thank-you note for coming and include 2–3 business cards with a small discount offer for your book on the back for them to give to family or friends. Make sure your discount has an expiration date in order to keep the book sales going on a regular basis.

That is it. Easy, fun, and profitable! Let your imagination roll and create The Ultimate Book Launch Party for you and your friends.[35]

If your release date is October 1 and you expect to have your books in hand a week or two before that, build in some extra time as a buffer. We had one author who was expecting to receive his books on December 1 (a Friday). He set up an autographing party and invited a lot of people for the following Monday. Wouldn't you know it; the truck carrying his books broke down in Phoenix, and they couldn't get the part needed to fix the truck until Monday morning. Fortunately, we had sent him five copies of the book on Thursday via overnight mail, so at least he had something to show the people who came!

Be prepared and be flexible. If your book is meant to glorify God and delivers on that desire, you will experience opposition. If it can go wrong, it will. So think ahead and don't plan events too close to the publication date.

Once your book has been published, it's time to fully implement your marketing strategy.

CHAPTER 9

How to Market Your Book

. . . .

WHEN YOU PROMOTE your book you are not promoting yourself, you are promoting the message God has given you!" These wise words, spoken by an author friend many years ago, have influenced my perspective on writing and publishing ever since.

Many people say they feel awkward about promoting their own book—they think it's prideful and pushy. I felt the same way when my first book came out, until my friend spoke those words. All of a sudden I was boldly talking about my book. You should be, too. If the Lord has given you a message to communicate, you needn't be shy about it. He wants you to get it to the people who need to hear it. The Lord's plan for your life and your book probably does not include a long-term lease on a dusty storage space.

Develop a Marketing Strategy

When you begin to think about your marketing plan, you need to ask yourself these questions: What problem does my book's message help people solve? Who needs to hear my message? Where can I find these people? How can I let them know about my book? Use the answers to these questions to effectively formulate your marketing strategy.

There are four basic ways to let people know about your book.

1. MEDIA EXPOSURE: radio, TV, print and Internet interviews; excerpts, articles, and reviews.

2. ADVERTISING: in trade publications; distributors' catalogs; magazines; niche newspapers; the Internet; and/or through direct mailings.

3. IN-PERSON PROMOTION: speaking engagements, book readings, and autograph parties.

4. TRADE SHOWS: setting up a booth at a trade show or convention, such as pastors' conventions or Sunday School workers' conferences.

We'll talk more about the different venues for promotion in the next chapter, but first, let's be sure you have the proper tools to present your product.

Create Marketing Tools That Stand Out

People are drawn to color. If all your marketing tools are created in black and white or one-color ink, their impact will be greatly diminished. That's why we always use the four-color process (full color) for our marketing tools.

Following are some of the most popular ways we've found to promote books:

1. FOUR-COLOR POSTCARDS (3.5 x 5.5 inches or giant-sized 6 x 9—keep in mind that the giant-size requires first class postage rather than the lower postcard rate).

2. FOUR-COLOR BOOKMARKS (1.5 x 7 inches). Readers love free bookmarks, and they're good advertising.

3. FOUR-COLOR BUSINESS CARDS (2 x 3 ½ inches; four-color on one side, black text on back). Some authors put their book cover on the full-color side and their name and ordering information on the other side. Pass them out everywhere.

4. FOUR-COLOR SALES FLIERS (8.5 x 11 inches; four-color, one side). List all pertinent ordering information on this flier so no matter how the person wants to order they will know how to go about it.

5. PROMOTIONAL ITEMS Pens, magnets, thumb drives, clocks, mugs, T-shirts, golf shirts, hats, gift bags, etc.

Publicity Kits

At WinePress, we design high-end, full-color publicity kits for our authors who sign up for a publicity package. Publicity kit materials are inserted into a full-color, high-gloss WinePress Publishing Group presentation folder that imitates our brand. When the media sees the green stripe and WP logo on the press kit, they know they are getting a quality product.

For the contents we use a high-quality paper stock that complements the folder. We create a one-sheet full-color summary that includes an author bio, book description, endorsements and positive comments, suggested interview questions, and a professionally-crafted press release.

Each polished, professional kit helps the author build credibility by creating a great first impression among industry or media representatives.

Tabletop Displays and Signs

You can find a great variety of tabletop displays that will give your book table a professional look. If you can secure a booth at a trade show—which will attract your buying public—you may want to invest in a trade-show-style tabletop display. My recommendation is either a tabletop or free-standing display from www.smartexhibits.com.

Now that you understand the importance of looking sharp, it's time to get your book out there so the world can see and hear the message God has given you.

CHAPTER 10

Creating a Demand for Your Book

· ·

YOU HAVE A message people need to hear. With the Lord's help and direction, you can create a demand for your book by exposing your message to as many markets as possible, in as many ways as possible. I can't say enough about developing a speaking ministry—if you have that gift and it is confirmed that the Lord wants you to move in that direction.

If you feel you need some training in this area, I recommend Christian Leaders, Authors & Speakers Services (CLASS). Their seminars are presented in major communities across the country by Marita Littauer, Florence Littauer, and other members of the teaching staff. CLASS seminars are usually structured as intensive, three-day sessions.

Speak Up with Confidence is another intensive Christian speaking seminar organized by Carol Kent of Speak Up Speaker Services. You might also consider joining a local Toastmasters group to polish your public speaking skills.

Self-published author, Sunie Levin, describes how she created a demand through her speaking ministry:

> When a computer search at my library revealed almost no books on how to develop a close grandparent/grandchild relationship, I decided to self-publish my first book, *Grandparents' Little Dividends: How to Keep in Touch*. I genuinely wanted to develop, in book form, my ideas on how to close the gap with my own seven grandchildren, particularly with the four that lived a considerable distance away from me. I also wanted to use the book in classes I'd be teaching in the fall. I knew that looking for a publisher was going to take time, more than I was willing to wait. I didn't even try to find a publisher. Here's how I went about the project.

First, I increased my visibility and credibility as a grandparent expert. I led seminars on grandparenting at local community centers, taught classes at local colleges, spoke to grandparents at retirement centers, churches, temples, and corporations. In short, I created valid credentials. I reached the point where the *Kansas City Star* dubbed me the "guru of grandparenting" in a feature article.

I spent six months collecting information on creative ways to make the grandparent/grandchild connection. I gave out surveys and networked with grandparent groups around the country.

Nine months later, the writing of my book was completed, and I joined a critique group. I took a few worthwhile suggestions and made my revisions . . . In 1989, I published my first 2,000 books at a production cost of $3.50 per book. The softcover book sold for $8 per copy. In less than one year, and with no advertising, I had sold all but 100 books.[36]

This author found that selling her book was easy because of her visibility at many speaking engagements.

Here are other avenues for creating a demand that you should prayerfully consider:

1. CHURCH LIBRARIANS. *Church Libraries*, a publication of the Evangelical Church Library Association (ECLA), no longer reviews self-published books because so many poorly-edited and designed self-published books were submitted. You can, however, send review copies of your book and promotional materials to individual church librarians. Many church librarians publish a library newsletter, or they review new books in the church's newsletter.

2. CHRISTIAN SCHOOL LIBRARIANS. If your book is appropriate for Christian school libraries, you will want to ask *The Christian Library Journal* to review your book. This publication is distributed to a large number of Christian school librarians, and it also accepts advertising.

3. MINISTRIES AND NONPROFIT ORGANIZATIONS. See if there are ministries or nonprofit organizations that might be interested in offering your book as a premium (fund-raiser giveaway). Depending on your topic, your local church may even be able to use it as a fund-raiser for their missions, youth, or other departments. You would have to give them a 50 to 70 percent discount, but you would be selling books by the case.

4. MAGAZINE SUBSCRIBERS. If your advertising budget allows, one great way of reaching a specific audience is to query magazines about using an excerpt—possibly allowing you to write the article—or having them write a book review. If any of these possibilities materialize, consider buying an ad in that issue. Keep in mind

that purchasing advertising does not guarantee sales. You may have seen our ads in World Magazine, Discipleship Journal, Pray, and Outreach, to name a few. These cooperative ads have been very successful in providing our authors with an affordable way to get great exposure for their books.

5. CHRISTIAN RADIO OR TV AUDIENCES. Your best shot at these markets is to launch a publicity campaign through a reputable Christian publicist. You must be a great communicator to be successful in this area. If your tendency is to speak in a monotone without much "pizzazz," then you'll probably be wasting your time and money trying this approach.

6. SECULAR RADIO OR TV AUDIENCES. If your book is geared to the general market, is not overtly Christian (i.e., it does not quote Scripture or use Christian jargon), and you are an effective communicator, your best way to get booked on radio and TV is through *Radio-TV Interview Report*. This magazine is read by many talk-show hosts and producers. The advertising is not overly expensive, and for the right topic, can be an effective way to reach the masses with your message.

7. THE SECULAR LIBRARY MARKET. The best way to reach this market is through Quality Books, a distributor to both public and school libraries. Though they buy your books on consignment at a steep discount, this is still a great way to get into that market.

8. ONLINE SERVICES/INTERNET. I understand that for every dollar you spend advertising on the Internet, you'll make $6 in sales. Utilizing appropriate keywords in Google adwords or earmarking advertising dollars for a campaign of banner ads on targeted sites can reap great rewards . . . that is, *if* you do your homework or work with a company with experience and know-how in this area. But advertising isn't the only way to take advantage of the Internet to get exposure for your book: there are Web sites, blogs, blog tours, virtual book tours, e-zines, articles on other Web sites, and more!

To help authors minimize the financial risk of testing new waters, all of our publishing packages include an automatic listing in our WinePress Online Bookstore as well as Amazon.com, BarnesandNoble.com, Christianbook.com, and others. The publishing packages include a dedicated Web page, full-color cover sample, book overview, and ability to order with a credit card. We also give our authors their own Weblog (blog), which ensures that keywords from their book are picked up by the major search engines.

One story that shows the value of key words dates back to mid-2001. We listed the key words "charmers" and "con-artists" for Sandra Scott's book, *Charmers & Con-Artists and Their Flip Side.* In 2004 we got a call from Sally Jesse Rafael's producer asking for Sandra to be the "expert" for a special show they were planning on con-artists. When we asked how they heard about Sandra and her book, they told us they typed "con-artists" into their search engine and up popped the information about Sandra's book. They flew her to New York, had her on the show, and she sold over 2,000 books as a result!

Our in-house publicity department works with our authors to help them find ways to market their books via the Internet. Here is an excerpt from our quarterly marketing newsletter, in which one of our publicists shared specific examples of how we use the Internet to benefit our authors:

> Rob Carmack recently completed *Box of Letters*, a collection of 96 devotionals written by a teenager for other teens. Obviously, teenagers comprise the target audience . . . see how easy this is! In the search engine Yahoo.com I typed in "Christian Youth Organizations." Excellent resources popped up such as Youth for Christ, Fellowship of Christian Athletes, Youth With a Mission, Young Life, Youthworkers.net, Youth Specialties, and a host of other great contacts.
>
> Where else do teenagers hang out? Christian summer camps, of course! The first camp I e-mailed immediately responded and asked for a review copy to consider as a resource. Here's an important tip: make sure you present your book as a helpful resource for their organizations' members. If they agree, their newsletter or other channels promote your book with little effort on your part.
>
> Doris Lyon, author of *My Personal Prayer Journal*, attends a Lutheran church. I went to Yahoo.com and typed in "Evangelical Lutheran Church." The first name on the list took me to elca.org. I then hit the "congregation" button and discovered that I could find all the Lutheran Churches within a 100 mile radius of a specified town, with a complete list of addresses and phone numbers. What a gold mine!
>
> David Leonardo battles with Multiple Sclerosis and his book, *Inspiration for Peace and Strength,* encourages people with long-term illnesses. The National Multiple Sclerosis Society Web site features a map of the United States with detailed local state chapter information. By making a few phone calls I discovered that most chapter program directors were willing to review the book and consider a newsletter article. Some even committed to give out a flyer to group leaders, who, in turn, let the members of their group know about David's book. BINGO! That's who we're trying to reach![37]

One other nifty idea that doesn't cost much money is an online service like America Online (AOL). You can find the message boards of people who would most likely be interested in your book. When you post at message boards, the key is to come up with the right wording for the subject line of your message. If the subject doesn't catch someone's eye, he or she will never bother to click on your item to read what's in the body of the message.

Other Internet resources for marketing your book include developing an online presence using social networking sites, Webcasts, and teleclasses. The opportunities are endless!

9. NARROWLY TARGETED MAILING LISTS. A few Christian companies specialize in selling the mailing lists of churches, ministries, people who have purchased a product out of XYZ Christian magazine, people who subscribe to XYZ Christian magazine, and so on. If you can narrow your target market to a category listed in one demographic base, you won't waste money mailing advertisements to people who haven't historically been interested in your topic. This is also true with e-mail lists that can be purchased from list companies.

10. CHRISTIAN BOOKSTORES VIA DISTRIBUTORS. With the right message, packaging, and marketing plan, it is possible to tap into the Christian bookstore market, especially when you have the help of a full-service publisher or book packager. With WinePress, you have the advantage of our contracts with all the major distributors, both Christian distributors and secular, as well as our presence in the Christian market. WinePress exhibits and aggressively promotes at the International Christian Retail Show each year in July and enables our authors unique exposure and networking to bookstore buyers and professionals in the industry.

11. CATALOGS FOR CHRISTIAN BOOKSTORE CUSTOMERS. When you see the large displays of books in chain stores, do you really think the store highlights those books out of the goodness of their hearts? No way. The publisher pays big bucks for those endcaps or face-out shelf space in the new release section. If you have a highly marketable product and a hefty advertising budget, you may want to consider an advertising campaign that targets the chain store catalogs. The ad could cost anywhere from $3,000 to $12,000 depending on the chain and the month you advertise. The nice thing about buying into a catalog like that is guaranteed sales. The bookstores that distribute the catalog ensure that they have stock on hand for all the products in the catalog. But again, being accepted is no easy feat. Your book has to really look good, and it has to *be* good. Each catalog has a committee to decide which titles should be accepted. Without the connections to these buyers and the protocol to present, success can be elusive . . . just another good reason to work with a team of professionals who have these kinds of relationships in the industry. One of our most recent success stories includes this type of advertising campaign. Catherine Hickem came to WinePress with her book *Raising Your Children with No Regrets* and the vision to take the book national. She budgeted enough to take a multi-pronged approach, one prong being

the Family Bookstore Catalog for Mother's Day, 2007. Since WinePress had an established relationship with the non-fiction buyer and knew the hoops to jump through, Family placed a significant order for her book and it sold well in their stores. Along with a Speaker Introduction Campaign where our staff presented her to MOPs groups and other churches in her area, and additional advertising to bookstore buyers, she sold over 7,500 copies in less than one year and was picked up by an agent. So, for the right book, with an author who is willing to take a risk to get their message out in a big way, catalogs and "guaranteed buys" into chain stores is a great option.

WinePress also offers our authors exposure to the bookstore market through our full-color catalog. We pay to send 4,500 copies (semi-annually) directly to bookstore buyers across the country.

12. MULTI-MEDIA PROMOTIONS. Utilizing video clips on your Web site is another great way to create demand for your book. Hosting clips of speaking engagements provides a connection that is often needed for a group to make the decision to book you for an event. Use technology to give Web site visitors an up-close and personal "look" at you, your book, and your message. Our multi-media department creates five-minute promotional DVDs for our authors. Our publicists oftentimes send them to larger TV stations and potential speaking venues to establish credibility and get the approval for the interview or engagement. This kind of cutting-edge technology is essential in building buzz and creating demand.

One last thing I'll mention before we move on is the importance of having your own Web site. While we offer our authors' books for sale on the WinePress Web site (www.winepressbooks.com), many authors have a more extended Web site, and they link to our site to offer their book for sale. Having your own Web site enables you to promote your book in a professional manner (as long as it has been designed by a professional and doesn't look too "mom & pop"). WinePress began its own Web design department a number of years ago, and we offer a wide variety of options for getting a Web site online quickly. For more information about our Web design services, visit http://www.wpisp.com.

Now it's time for the distribution end of things. Let's see how we can get your well-marketed book to your waiting customer in the fastest, most professional manner.

CHAPTER 11

Making Your Book Available

· ·

L ET'S ADDRESS ONE of the biggest challenges for the self-published author: making your book available to those who need to read it. If you think most people are going to take the time to write a check, lick a stamp, address an envelope, and run to the mailbox in order to get your book, you need to wake up and smell the coffee. Most people will do one of three things to get their hands on a Christian book: call a toll-free number to order it with a credit card, go online to order (which is the #1 way people order nowadays), or stop by their favorite Christian bookstore.

If you seek a wide audience or national recognition, you need to prayerfully consider the following proven methods of helping the general public obtain your book:

Christian Bookstores

While it's difficult to break into the national market, you may do well with your local independent Christian bookstores. Some may be willing to purchase small quantities of your book for a 40 percent discount. Others may take them on consignment. Unfortunately, since larger corporations are buying up many of the small Christian bookstores, buyers are often times no longer employed at the local level. Purchasing is normally done in large quantities, at large discounts, directly from the big publishers and distributors, with orders placed by the corporate office of the bookstore chain.

Many bookstores offer a service called Quest. At a kiosk in the store, the customer can use a touch-screen to look up an author, artist, or keyword and find any book, video, music tape, CD, Bible, gift, or resource available through distributors to that bookstore.

The customer can also view the front and back cover and table of contents, listen to sound bytes of music, or watch clips from a video. This service is available in the local bookstore in downtown Enumclaw, and it is a great way to allow customers to find the product they desire and special order it if it is not in stock. At WinePress, we submit all the information about our authors' books to the Quest database so our books are easily found at bookstores throughout the country.

Another unique advantage to working with WinePress is our latest product launch. At the 2008 ICRS Convention in Orlando, we introduced a new gourmet book themed coffee product for our sister company, "Book Brew Coffee." Nearly 200 retailers attended the free breakfast event to taste test the new blends, Writer's Roast, Reader's Choice, Dictionary Decaf, Bestseller's Blend, Breakfast Preface, and Editor's Select. This is a proprietary gourmet product distributed by WinePress. The response has been incredible, with coffee connoisseurs from across the country giving the product rave reviews. This brings more retailers direct to us for product, which gives our authors greater exposure and the opportunity to sell their books at a lower discount than the distributors require.

Christian Book Distributors

As I've stressed throughout this book, chances of your book landing on a bookstore shelf are slim. The Christian bookstore market is so competitive that your book must have national appeal (i.e., no poetry, missionary stories, or general testimonies—unless you are famous). Your book must be extremely well-written and have sufficient dollars behind it to support large advertising and media campaigns. Most Christian book distributors won't look at your book if:

a. They know you've self-published on your own

b. You're not an established author

I've discovered a few ways around this avenue that can be beneficial to WinePress authors (another good reason to publish with WinePress). We have contracts with all the major distributors, who purchase our authors' books at a 50–55 percent discount (as opposed to the 60 percent discount plus freight costs that many small publishers pay to their distributors). Our distributor pays the freight and we do some extra promotion by sending our catalog to all the bookstore buyers twice a year, as well as passing out our catalog at the annual International Christian Retail Show.

Recently, we contracted with a sales force who sold our titles to bookstores nationwide; we found that they over-promised and under-delivered. We have concluded that the best bet for a self-published author is to see the bookstore market as gravy, not as the primary outlet for your book. Unless, of course, you are willing to commit significant dollars to market to the chain stores, as mentioned in the last chapter.

Fulfillment

The best way to make your book easily available to the general public is through a fulfillment service, which allows customers to order your book via credit card by calling a toll-free number. The service includes warehousing the inventory, answering the phone, taking orders, and shipping the product. As detailed in chapter 5 on Industry Terms, the average amount you'll pay for this kind of service is 35 to 65 percent of the retail price of the book. Our charge at WinePress is anywhere from 20 percent up to 35 percent for order taking, credit card processing, billing, collection, bad checks, declined credit cards, mis-routed packages, lost or damaged shipments, insured inventory, etc.

I developed this service many years ago because, as an author, I didn't want to hassle with this kind of work and I knew other authors wouldn't want to, either. For my first printing of *Consumed by Success*, I fulfilled my orders through a secular company. When all was said and done, I paid just over 50 percent of the book price for that service. They charged me for every little thing, including warehousing, insurance, inquiry calls (which do not necessarily turn into orders), charge-card fees, order fees, administrative fees, and so on. They are, however, a reputable company, and I felt the service was a valuable one. When I was a guest on the Prime Time America show with Jim Warren on the Moody Network, we gave out the toll-free number and sold over 700 copies of my book in an afternoon. So it was important to have a company that could handle that kind of volume. I was certainly glad to have someone else taking those calls and handling the orders.

As you research fulfillment services, be sure to ask how many operators they have on duty. Some have only a few people answering the phones. If you land a syndicated radio interview, your service might not be able to handle all the calls. Every lost call is a lost sale. Also, be sure to request a statement of charges ahead of time to learn what will be covered.

I finally became so discouraged with what was available out there that I established a fulfillment service for WinePress authors. We are set up to be able to go from 7 operators on call to 35 operators if the situation demands it. We don't nickel-and-dime people to death; instead, we keep costs to a reasonable amount.

One great success story happened when Dan Miller appeared on the Hour of Power show with Dr. Robert Schuller. He did a 20-minute interview, and Dr. Schuller gave out our toll free number about 10 times during the interview. Within four days we had about

2,500 orders for Dan's book, *Living, Laughing and Loving Life!* Even with the normal fulfillment charge, the income he generated from that one show actually paid for the entire print run of 10,000 books.

Book Table

During speaking engagements, your book table at the back of the room is your primary means for making books available. Be sure the table looks good, with professionally-produced signs and a handsome display of your books. You can usually find inexpensive, tabletop plate holders at craft shops and dollar stores to display your book in a way that looks sharp. Be prepared with lots of change, and keep several pens handy—people will ask you to autograph your book!

Order Information

Place your ordering information on the first available right-hand page that follows the last text or reference section of your book. Confused? See our order page at the end of this book. And be sure to check out the laws in your state. Most states require that you establish a business license and a resale account with the Department of Revenue, since you are purchasing your books at a wholesale price and reselling them at a retail price.

When you sell to someone who lives in your state, you usually have to charge them the appropriate sales tax. As of 2009, you don't have to charge sales tax when you sell to someone who is out of state, but I understand that's about to change as well. The simplest way to handle the bookkeeping is to keep track of the amount you take in for sales tax and set it aside in a savings account. Then, once a quarter or once a year when you have to fill out the paperwork to pay your sales taxes, you've got the money in hand.

CHAPTER 12

Getting the Most Out of the Media

• •

THE MEDIA IS a great asset in generating exposure for your book. Publicist Don Otis, from Veritas Communications, has given me permission to edit and reprint some incredibly detailed and important publicity how-to information he has compiled but never published.

Part I: Getting Started

Language and Words: Using Words Effectively to Communicate Your Message

The goal of communication is to impart what you know or believe to your audience. This means selecting the words you use very carefully. Jesus used stories, parables, and allegories to communicate in ways that His hearers could understand. The words you choose can be powerful. They can also be dangerous. The art of using words to persuade is called rhetoric. This is a basic part of scholarly discipline. It is also necessary if you want to communicate your message. By using words in certain ways, we can manipulate people to do just about anything. Hitler is proof enough. His two most potent weapons were sloganeering and repetition.

Author Steve Brown says, "The goal of communication is not to impress, but to communicate clearly." And a major element of clear communication is simplicity. Cleverly chosen language has the effect of simplifying ideas rather than complicating them. Intellectualizing often confuses the listener instead of imparting ideas, concepts, or information. As writer E. B. White said, "Avoid the elaborate, the pretentious, the coy, and the cute."

Language has been called the greatest drug known to humanity. Jesus said that our words justify or condemn us (Matt. 12:37). The way we use words, and how we define them, has an effect not just on what we think but on how we think. Politicians, social engineers, and the military are clever in cloaking the true meaning of their words in euphemisms. They obscure realities we'd rather not deal with. For example, "collateral damage" refers to civilian casualties. When the military "re-deploys troops," it often means retreat. Our prison system uses "honor ranches" in place of prisons and "boys' homes" rather than juvenile detention. Each of these is an example of hiding the truth with words.

Words are powerful. They are so powerful that God confused languages to control the effect words had on the human race. Words put into languages are the most complex creation of the human mind. Babel is testament to the creative power and influence of words. God used words to create the world and all that it contains (Ps. 33:6). By our words we can create and build. And by our words we can dismantle or inflict pain. It is not by accident that the countries with the most advanced technology also have the fewest languages. And the world's 6,000 languages are gradually disappearing. This global language extinction is leading us back to the place where communication was first scrambled in Babel.

Expectations

Working with a publicist will help you get the most out of your publishing experience. Even before your book is off the press, the work to promote it has begun. Once it is off the press, promotion moves into a more aggressive mode. Publicists view the promotion of your book as a joint venture. By this I mean a positive author-publicity relationship will ensure that your book gets the best media coverage. Your participation in the media and promotion process will directly influence the sales and success of your book.

Here is what you can expect from a good publicist.
They will . . .

- Write and prepare press materials. These are written to attract the attention of a host or producer. They do not try to portray every major aspect of your book.

- Prepare questions for your interviews.

- Mail information about your book to appropriate media sources.

- Provide a review copy of your book to interested media.

- Work with you to schedule media opportunities.

- Send review copies of your book to book reviewers.

- Send review copies to key influencers and opinion makers.

- Provide "coaching" help for interviews.

Publicists do not . . .

- Handle the shipping or mailing of your books for special meetings or events.

- Serve as a public speaking agency.

- Place space ads in magazines or newspapers.

Side note: While this last statement made by Don Otis is typically true, it is not the case with WinePress. Our in-house publicists place space ads and facilitate the creative copy writing and design aspects of the ad, acting in many ways as a full fledged advertising agency. With our Speaker Introduction Campaign, we make cold calls to churches or groups in your area to introduce you as a possible speaker. And, for many of our authors who have a thriving speaking ministry, we ship books from our warehouse to their speaking engagements across the United States and to other countries as well. However, working with a typical freelance Christian publicist, these opportunities are, as Don states, not an option.

Publicity: What Is It?

We define publicity broadly to mean "any reasonable opportunity to gain public exposure for an author to promote their product." The idea is to attract public interest in your book. A good publicist focuses most available resources in three main areas: radio, television, and print media.

Radio

There are more than 1,300 Christian radio stations scattered throughout the United States. Christian radio now represents the nation's third largest format. Many of these stations have regional talk shows. A good publicist will use whatever creative means available to position you for an appearance on these regional or national programs. It is a publicist's job to secure airtime for you. It is your job to promote your book or product. Most radio talk programs fall into issue-related classifications like family, theology, politics, or current events.

Let's take a brief look at some characteristics of radio interviews. Your interviews will last between 15 minutes and one hour. Most interviews can be done by phone from your home or office. Radio interviews will be either taped or live. When your publicist confirms an interview with you, the form will tell you which it is.

- Radio is fast moving. Be prepared to respond as quickly as possible to questions.

- Some live radio programs open phone lines for callers.

- Radio is personal. Though many people are listening at any given time, you are being heard by one person at a time. Individuals are listening in their cars, on the job, or at home.

- Radio is an effective tool for communicating your message.

- Some radio hosts will be excited by or sympathetic with your topic. Others may disagree or sound disinterested.

Here are a few items to remember when you're doing an interview:

- Be enthusiastic. Be positive and energetic.

- Be relational. Try to identify with the host or the city you are being heard in.

- Use short examples, stories, or research findings to bolster your main points.

- Keep a marked-up copy of your book close by. Flag the pages you might quote from.

- Be on time.

- Be prepared. If you use notes, keep them close by. For call-in programs, we suggest you keep a notepad nearby. Write down the names of callers so you can respond to them by name.
- Keep a glass of water nearby.

- If you are doing a phone interview, be sure to eliminate any distractions ahead of time. Find a quiet place away from children or noise. If you have call waiting on your phone, have it turned off during your interviews.
- Listen to the questions carefully and respond appropriately and you'll do fine.
- Be timely. If your book or product can be tied to a particular current event, use it.
- Be courteous to the host and callers.
- Be gracious. Be sure to thank the host for having you on.

Now that we've covered what you should do, let's look at what you should avoid during a radio interview.

- Avoid euphemisms. This is a Greek word meaning "using auspicious words." Make yourself understandable to as many people as possible.

- Avoid using legal terms (unless you explain what they mean and they are relevant to the interview).

- Avoid theological terms (same rule applies).

- Avoid medical or psychological terms.

- Don't insult your host either directly or indirectly.

- Do not assume people know what you're talking about. No one knows your book (or subject) as well as you. Your tendency will be to assume that the people listening know more than they do. A word of caution: Be careful not to patronize or talk down to the host or audience just because you do know more.

- Don't use clichés.

- Avoid name dropping.

- Do not embellish or exaggerate.

- Avoid gossip or talking down about others.

- Be careful not to "over promote" yourself. Some hosts will cut you off immediately if they feel you're using their show as an extended commercial.

Television

There are fewer than 200 Christian television programs in the United States. While most of these are regional, some, like The 700 Club, are national. Television is distinctive because it engages several senses at the same time. Television is very different from radio because you have to be there to do the interview. That's why it's important that you let your publicist know about any travel plans you may have as far in advance of a trip as possible. Sometimes your publicist can schedule you on television during your travel.

Here are some things to remember when doing television interviews:

- Avoid bright colors, especially white.

- Respond to the host rather than looking toward the camera.

- Arrive early for television tapings.

- Don't take notes with you.

- Bring at least one or two copies of your book with you.

- Bring a set of questions.

- Body language is important on TV. Don't slouch or fidget. Never assume the camera is not on you.

Print

Books, newspapers, and magazines are the primary print media. The print media fall into several classifications: Christian tabloids, Christian magazines, secular newspapers and magazines, and ministry newsletters or magazines. In each case; remember who you are talking to. Be relevant. If you do an interview with a secular publication, learn as much as you can beforehand about the person who is interviewing you. Try to find out the angle they are looking for. What can you find out about their own beliefs? How will they use them? Have they interviewed anyone else on the subject? Use words sparingly and use them carefully when talking with secular journalists.

Usually your publicist works to obtain book reviews on every title they represent. This does not mean that every book will be reviewed in major publications. However, some local secular newspapers and Christian newspapers will review your book. Sometimes when review copies of your book are sent out, a publication will decide to run an excerpt. If you have contacts with either local Christian or secular print media, let your publicist know. Your publicist will work with your local newspapers.

Publicity: What You Can Do

Typically, authors believe their job is over when their book goes to press. As mentioned before, promotion is a team effort. Even during the height of a publicity campaign there are things you can do to provide an extra publicity boost.

- Always carry a couple copies of your book with you. If you travel, keep one in your car or carry-on bag.

- Introduce yourself to local bookstore owners or buyers. If they are not carrying your book, ask them to.

- Ask your friends or family living in different areas to call their local bookstores and ask them to carry your book.

- If you do public speaking, be sure to have plenty of copies of your book on hand for your meetings. Most churches will provide someone to handle a book table for you. If you're invited to speak at a church meeting or seminar, ask the host to provide a table. When speaking publicly, be sure to mention the availability of your book.

Part Two: The Interview Process

Working with Your Publicist: Getting the Most Out of Your Media Campaign

What is a media campaign? Most would define a campaign as a four- to six-month effort to provide the greatest possible media exposure for your book. Here are a few quick tips to help you work effectively with your publicist.

- Provide a travel itinerary.

- Provide a list of the best or worst times for doing interviews.

- Respond quickly. An interview can be lost when an author takes too much time to respond to an interview opportunity. If you are exceptionally busy, provide your publicist with "the holes in your schedule" and they'll do their best to work with you. If you have done interviews before, let them know about it. It is easier to go back to "good interviewers" and avoid those who were unpleasant. If you have contacts with any media, let your publicist know about them.

- If you have specific questions you want to be asked about your book, be sure to let your publicist know before they put your prepared questions together.

- They can do a better job for you if you take the time to let them know your ideas up front.

A Typical Interview: What Can I Expect?

If you've never done a media interview before, don't worry. Just remember, you're the expert! After you've done several interviews you will find yourself repeating many of the same things. You will also discover there are good and bad interviewers. The best interviews are those where the person who interviews you has actually read your book. However, sometimes you will find hosts who have just skimmed your materials. Once in a while, you will find yourself in an interview with a host who hardly remembers your name! If this happens, take control of the interview by discussing your book or topic. In many instances, this will bring relief to a host and salvage an otherwise wasted interview.

A typical interview includes at least three sections: an opening (this is where having a good bio is important), the body of the interview (the content), and the close (the wrap-up). If you are on a live call-in program, a fourth ingredient will include the callers.

The opening is important since it sets the stage for both the host and the listeners (or viewers). The introduction establishes your credibility to say what you have to say.

If this is done ineffectively, you can recall your credentials without sounding arrogant. For example, "While I was conducting my research at Harvard, I discovered . . ." Or, "When I studied law the two things I found most disturbing were . . ." If a host has your biography and does his or her job well, you can stick to the subject.

The body of the interview will generally follow one of two directions: The interviewer will use the prepared questions or he or she will use a more spontaneous approach. A good host will gently challenge your assumptions by asking questions anyone in the audience would ask if they were there. Don't be offended by the "devil's advocate" questions. These do not necessarily mean a host disagrees with you. The close of the interview should consist of a brief recap of what your book is about. It must also include a mention of the book and where listeners can get a copy . . . The onus is on you, not the host. If the book has not been mentioned, you might ask (on the air), "May I mention where your listeners (viewers) can find my book?" If you have time before the interview, ask the host if you can mention where to find the book.

A final word about the interview process. You will find some radio interviews are on commercial stations and some are on noncommercial stations. On commercial stations you can expect frequent interruptions (every 7 to 12 minutes) for a commercial break. Use this time to gather your thoughts and prepare for the next segment. Interviews on noncommercial stations will generally have few if any interruptions.

Preparing for an Interview: What You Should Know

There is an English proverb that says, "Hope for the best, but prepare for the worst." Just like any other job, interviewers have good days and bad days. If you happen to hit one on a bad day, try to make the best of your time. And just as interviewers have bad days, so do authors. Authors don't do interviews for a living, so the likelihood of something going wrong is even greater. This shouldn't scare you but it should keep you on your toes. The best interviews are with authors who are rested and alert.

Your interview will be as successful as you are prepared—mentally and spiritually.

What to avoid during an interview

The best advice I can offer is to "be yourself." Be who you are without any pretense. Be natural and relaxed. Too much anxiety will rob you of your ability to think clearly. However, having said this, a little fear can also be a good thing. It is also very normal. Author Steve Brown calls fear "a wonderful motivator." It can be an encouragement to keep you mentally alert.

Here are some tips to help you relax:

- Imagine that you are talking with only one person.

- Take a deep breath before you go on the air and during any commercial breaks.

- Take a moment to pray before you go on the air. If you can, pray with the host—this is even better.

- Know your material. You are at an advantage because it is your material you're discussing. Don't be led into discussions on topics you don't know anything about. If you are an expert on "home schooling," don't be pulled into a discussion about "How to discipline children." If you find yourself "off track," don't be afraid to say something like, "I'm sure there are better qualified people to discuss that subject, but I can tell you more about . . ." This can get you and the host back on track and away from things that are unconnected to your book.

- Finally, don't act bored by the interview. If you're bored, chances are good that the audience and host will also be bored. Enthusiasm can make even the most trivial conversations seem more interesting. Frank Sinatra once said to his son, "Don't ever let me catch you singing like that again, without enthusiasm. You're nothing if you're not excited about what you're doing."

What to remember during an interview

The most important thing to remember is that you don't have to be perfect to be effective. Keep your answers simple. Keep them short. Remember that your job is to hook the listener so that he will want to know more about what you have to say. You don't have to cover everything in your book in a 30-minute interview. That's not possible anyway. If you feel pressed for time, you can say, "I cover this issue more fully in chapter 7 of my book . . ."

The beginning of your interview is like the beginning of a speech. Your audience will make a quick judgment about whether they want to listen to you. Your opening comments will set the stage for anything else you have to say. In his book, *How to Talk So People Will Listen* (Baker Books), Steve Brown offers the following dos and don'ts for speeches. They are equally applicable for media interviews.

- Don't apologize. Do not say, "I haven't done very many interviews before so I'm rather nervous." If you are doing an interview by phone, just pretend you're having a normal conversation with a friend.

- Don't demean. The audience is giving you their time. You owe them something. Don't insult them.

- Don't patronize. The audience will tune you out if you come across as arrogant.

- Do get the listener's attention. Start by citing something to perk the audience's attention. This can include a piece of research, a quote, or simply an enticing opening comment.

- Do whet the listener's appetite. Asking the listeners a question is a good way to keep them thinking. You can "bait" and keep an audience by saying something like, "I'll explain this in further detail later, but first . . ."

- Do give the listeners your theme. Be sure you state and restate what your book is about. Ask yourself, "Why would a person want to hear what I have to say?"

Afterward: What to do when you hang up the phone

Some authors actually take notes during an interview. This makes sense if you want to remember names or keep on track during the interview. They are also very helpful to use . . . if you write the interviewer a note of thanks. Most of us are like the nine lepers who after they were healed by Jesus went on their way. Set yourself apart by sending a brief note of thanks to the interviewer. The form your publicist sends you to notify you about your interview will have the name and address of the person you do the interview with.

Part III: Interview Tactics and Questions

How to Promote Your Book without Sounding Like a Commercial

Many of us have difficulty promoting ourselves. That's normal. The trick is to find ways that accomplish your purpose (promoting your book) without sounding like an infomercial. It's actually much easier than you might think.

If you do an adequate job of creating an appetite for your book, the host will be more assertive in asking you where your book can be purchased. The better you are at tantalizing the listeners, the greater the motivation to buy your book. For example, let's say you have a book called *Seven Godly Principles to a More Fulfilling Marriage*. If you simply give all these principles away during an interview, the listener has no need to buy your book. A smart way to create interest is with a comment or phrase. Using the example above, you might say something like, "My fifth principle has to do with sex, but it's not what you think." This statement creates more curiosity or a desire to know more.

The most difficult thing most authors face is how to promote their book during an interview. The interview itself should take care of this dilemma. As you are asked specific questions, answer them succinctly without going into too much detail. Use the end of your comment to say something like "I wish we had time to go into further detail on this, but if you'd like more information on this you can find it in chapter 3 of my book." This does not sound overly promotional but does leave the listener with the idea that he is far better off to get the book if he wants to know more.

Depending on the availability of your book, you'll want to encourage listeners to call your toll-free number rather than going to their local bookstore to purchase your book.

Diplomacy: How to Handle Tricky Questions

There are several useful rules for handling tricky or difficult questions during an interview. If you remember these rules, you can get out of almost any tough situation.

- RULE #1: You don't have to answer every question. This may sound odd if you're doing an interview. However, there will be some questions that are not relevant to your book. If they are "out of bounds," don't be afraid to say so. For example, "I wish I had an answer to that question myself!"

- RULE #2: You are not an expert on everything. Isn't that a relief? If you don't have an answer, don't pretend you do. There is nothing wrong with saying "I don't know." You will get into far more trouble trying to answer questions you know nothing about.

- RULE #3: Don't argue with the host. This does not mean you can't disagree. The key word here is argue. This will quickly destroy an interview. How do you avoid arguments? One of the simplest ways is to ignore statements you might otherwise feel compelled to correct. If it is important, disagree with it. If you do, be willing to cite your reasons, research, or sources. Remember the old adage, "The customer is always right." The same rule applies to interviews, unless the host is stealing your wallet!

- RULE #4: Diversion is the best method to avoid confrontation. If you are asked a question you don't want to answer, then answer something else. What do you do if the host asks you, "Have you beaten your wife lately?" Since no answer is a good answer, you might respond by saying, "That's a good question, but what my book is really about is how to minimize the effects of violence in the family."

Live Shows: What to Do With Annoying Callers

The job of the producer is to screen callers. The job of a good host is to keep the interview from getting off track. It's their job to control the interview. Callers often have their "own agenda." If the host doesn't keep things on track, then don't be afraid to do it yourself. A caller may ask, "Do you believe that UFOs are sent from the devil?" If your subject is about marriage, you might say, "I have no idea, but I would be glad to answer any questions about marriage."

There are different types of callers. They are lonely, argumentative, fixated (on some subject other than yours!) and those who really are interested. You never know for sure which one you'll have until they're on the line. But that's what makes talk radio so interesting.

You must immediately assess which category the caller falls into. If someone wants to argue, don't argue back. Try to be soft and gentle without compromising your position. The key is to pacify the caller. When you use an angry caller's first name, that can work wonders to soothe his anger. For example, "Steve, that's your name, isn't it? I know you're frustrated by what I've said, but please try to see it from a different perspective." In almost every instance you can win the heart of a caller by identifying with them in some way. This is not just clever manipulation but show[s] genuine interest in them or the difficulty they're facing.

Five Questions Authors Ask Most

1. Do interviews really sell books? The answer is yes. They are second only to public endorsements from others or your own meetings.

2. How many interviews will I do? The answer to this question depends upon the subject of your book. The range of interviews is anywhere from twenty to seventy interviews, with thirty to thirty-five being about average.

3. What if I need to cancel an interview? If you cannot do an interview that has already been scheduled, call your publicist right away. Don't wait until the last minute.

4. Can I get a copy of my interview? In most cases the answer is yes. Let the host know in advance that you want a copy of the interview. If you are doing a television taping, take an extra video cassette along with you.

5. When will I be on Focus on the Family, The 700 Club or Oprah? The larger the program the harder it is to schedule an interview. For example, The 700 Club receives 300 to 400 program suggestions every week. With only five or ten guest openings per week, they schedule between 1 and 3 percent of the program ideas they receive.

Part IV: Speaking from Experience

What Makes a Good Interview: A Host's Perspective

"I look for someone who can bring a biblical perspective to an issue. I want them to focus on a real life issue."

—Bill Feltner, KNIS Radio

"An author needs to be able to express the essence of their book. I like an author who will deliberately connect with me as a person."

—*Ron Reed, Lifetime Radio*

"The author should always be more prepared for an interview because there is no guarantee the host will grasp all the content. Always provide a solid, firm answer to a question. Keep it simple for the audience. Remember that your personality is a turn on or turn off to the listener."

—*John Young, WNIV Radio*

Some Final Advice From Talk-Show Hosts

- Send a thank-you note.

- Don't assume the audience knows who you are. Most people have probably never heard about you before.

- Don't over-promote your book.

- Every interview is a new interview. If you act disinterested, it will turn off the audience.

- Ask for a copy of your interview and then critique it. Ask yourself, "Would I listen to myself?"

- Make sure the audience knows your name. If they can't remember the title of your book, they may remember your name.

- Make sure the listener knows how to get a copy of your book.

Epilogue

. . . .

I HOPE THIS book has encouraged you to move ahead with publishing the message God has given you. I trust it has informed you about your options and empowered you to prayerfully make the right decision.

This book is meant to augment other, more detailed books on self-publishing and to amplify the specifics as they relate to the Christian market. While many of the books I have recommended are excellent, they cite secular resources for advertising, distribution, and other facets of publishing. This won't do you any good if you've written a book with an overtly Christian message; thus, the need for information geared to the Christian writer. I hope you now feel confident that indeed, you can get your message into print in a way that will truly glorify God.

I'd like to close with the following quotation, from a tract published by Pilgrim Tract Society. The author is unknown, but I am sure it will encourage you to keep on keepin' on!

Your Work

The Lord has given to every man his work. It is his business to do it—and the devil's business to hinder him if he can. So, sure as God has given you a work to do, Satan will try to hinder you. He may present other things more promising, he may allure you by worldly prospects, he may assault you with slander, torment you with false accusations, set you to work defending your character, employ pious persons to lie about you, editors to assail you, and excellent men to slander you. You may have Pilate, Herod, Annas, and Caiaphas all combined against you, and Judas standing by ready to sell you for thirty pieces of silver. You may wonder why all these things come upon you. Can you not see that the whole thing is brought about through the craft of the devil to draw you off from your work and hinder your obedience to God?

Keep about your work. Do not flinch because the lion roars; do not stop to stone the devil's dogs; do not fool away your time chasing the devil's rabbits. Do your work. Let liars lie, let sectarians quarrel, let corporations resolve, let editors publish, let the devil do his worst; but, see to it that nothing hinders you from fulfilling the work that God has given you.

He has not sent you to make money. He has not commanded you to get rich. He has never bidden you to defend your character. He has not set you at work to contradict falsehoods that Satan and his servants may start to peddle. If you do these things, you will do nothing else; you will be at work for yourself and not for the Lord.

Keep about your work. Let your aim be as steady as a star. Let the world brawl and bubble. You may be assaulted, wronged, insulted, slandered, wounded, and rejected; you may be abused by foes, forsaken by friends, and despised and rejected of men; but see to it with steadfast determination, with unfaltering zeal, that you pursue the great purpose of your life and the object of your being until at last you can say, "I have finished the work which Thou gavest me to do." Amen.[38]

In parting, I'll leave you with just one word of caution. We often think our message is from God when in reality it is just "self" speaking loud and clear. I encourage you to get into the prayer closet and seek the Living God to make sure what you have is from Him. If it is, then be obedient to get the message out, no matter what the obstacles!

Endnotes

Chapter 1

1. Smietana, Bob, "Looking for the Next Big Thing," *Christianity Today* (June, 2007).

2. St. Lifer, Evan. "2005 Book Prices," *School Library Journal,* www.schoollibraryjournal. com/article/CA507329.html

3. "Real Writers Losing Out on Contracts," *Dallas Morning News* (July 26, 1997).

4. "2005 Book Prices."

5. *Book Trends 2003,* CBA Marketplace (March 2003).

6. Hansen, Collin, "What's Not Coming to a Bookstore Near You, How competition to publish celebrity Christians crowds out theology" *Christianity Today* (9/14/2007), www.christianitytoday.com/ct/2007/septemberweb-only/137-52.0.html

7. *The Written Word,* WinePress Publishing, (vol. 1, no. 1, Summer 1995), 6–7.

8. Veith, Gene Edward, "Whatever Happened to Christian Publishing?" *WORLD* magazine (July 12/19, 1997), 13–15.

9. Hansen, Collin, "What's Not Coming to a Bookstore Near You. How competition to publish celebrity Christians crowds out theology" *Christianity Today* (9/14/2007), www.christianitytoday.com/ct/2007/septemberweb-only/137-52.0.html

10. "Real Writers Losing Out on Contracts," *Dallas Morning News* (July 26, 1997).

11. Baue, F.W., "Publishing, Perishing," *WORLD* magazine (July 4, 1998).

12. "Whatever Happened to Christian Publishing?" Gene Edward Veith, *WORLD* magazine (July 12 / 19, 1997), 13–15.

13. IBID.

14. Armstrong, John, "Viewpoint: A Look at Reformation & Revival in Our Time," quoted by Gene Edward Veith in "Whatever Happened to Christian Publishing," *WORLD* magazine (July 12/19, 1997), 13–15.

15. Connor, Tom, "The State of the Industry," *Writer's Digest* (January 2006).

16. "Not-by-the-Books," *U.S. News & World Report* (vol. 112, no. 22, June 8, 1992), 73.

17. IBID.

18. Poynter, Dan, *The Self-Publishing Manual* (Santa Barbara, CA: Para Publishing, 9th ed., 1996), 25–28.

19. Poynter, Dan and Mindy Bingham, *Is There a Book Inside of You?* (Santa Barbara, CA: Para Publishing, 4th ed., 1997), 26–27.

Chapter 2

20. Stuart, Sally, *Advanced Christian Writer,* (November–December, 2001), 11.

21. IBID.

22. Stuart, Sally, *The Written Word,* (February 2005).

23. *The Written Word,* WinePress Publishing, (vol. 1, no. 1, Summer 1995), 6–7.

24. "Self-Publishing Successes," *Publishers Weekly* (May 22, 1995).

25. "Books for the Asking," *New York Times* (October 17, 2002).

Chapter 4

26. Crosby, Cindy, "Advancing the Cause" *Publishers Weekly* (December 8, 2008), 27

27. *The Self-Publishing Manual,* 16, 19, 22–25.

28. IBID.

29. IBID.

30. IBID.

31. IBID.

32. Shatzkin, Mike, "15 Trends to Watch in 2008," *Publishers Weekly* (Jan. 7, 2008), 22.

33. "Can You Curl Up With a Good E-Book Reader?" *Consumer Reports* (Feb. 2008), 9.

34. Excerpt from a letter from the acquisitions editor, *** Publishers (Feb. 28, 1996).

Chapter 7

35. Lopez, Clary, "The Ultimate Book Launch Party." Clary is the CEO/Founder of Guerrilla Marketers Café, a book promotion site. She is an author, moderator and publicist. She is preparing to launch her next book, *BookPromo Year 1*. You can contact her at guerrilla@clarylopez.com or visit her Web sites http://guerrilla.clarylopez.com, http://bookhomestead.com and her official author site http://clarylopez.com.

Chapter 9

36. "Self-Publishing Technique," *Writer's Digest* (vol. 74, no. 11, November 1994), 36.
37. WinePress Partnership Newsletter (vol. 3, issue 1, Winter 2001).

Epilogue

38. "Keep at Your Work!" Trivium Pursuit, http://www.triviumpursuit.com/blog/2005/12/20/keep-at-your-work/

LaVergne, TN USA
07 June 2010
185145LV00004B/3/P

9 781414 112442